ENGLISH OMEGA

THE PRINCIPLES AND ELEMENTS OF ART

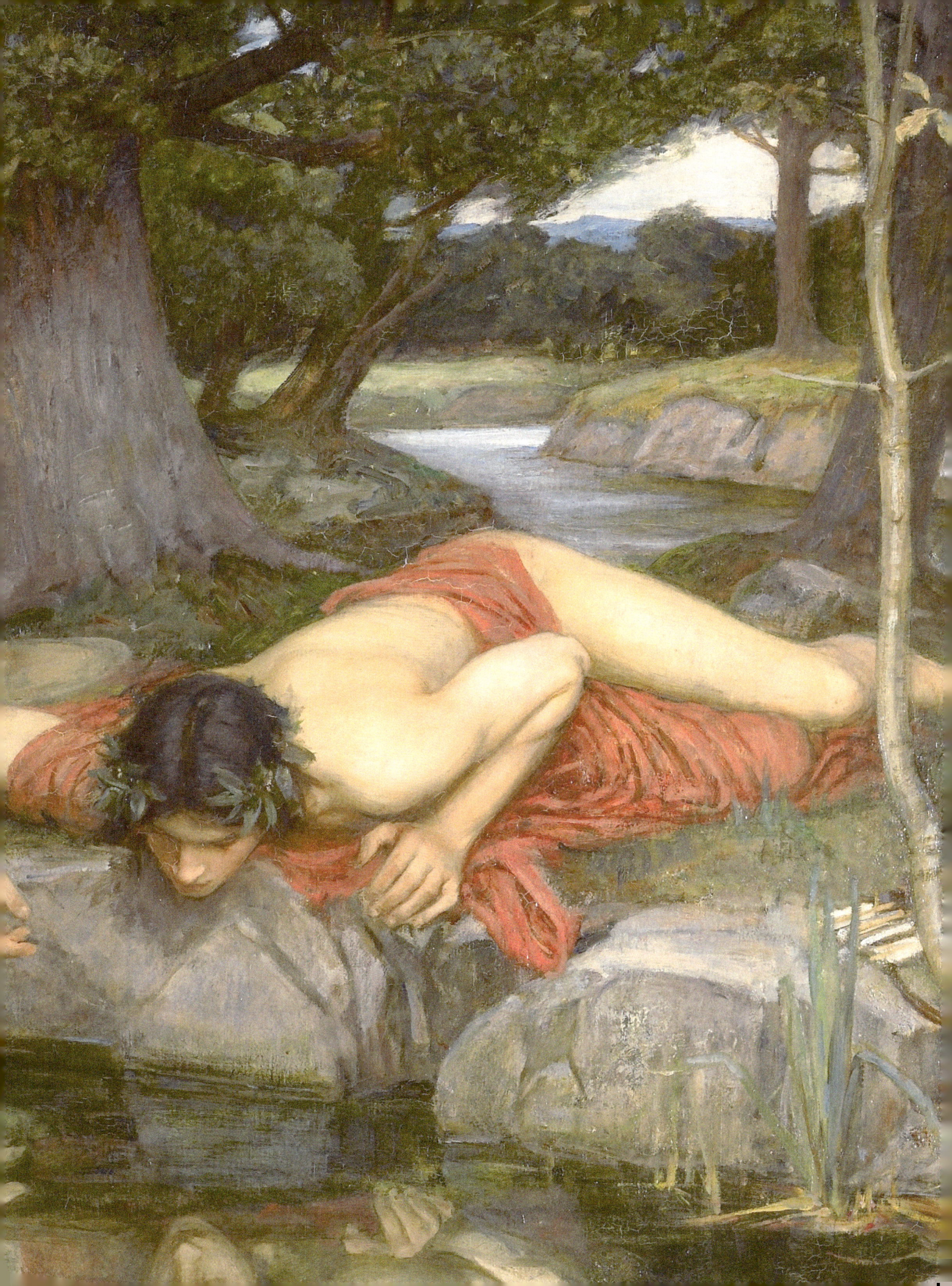

UNIT	FEATURED ARTIST	CRITICAL THINKING
Unit 1 **Balance**	EDVARD MUNCH	Back to Balance
Unit 2 **Rhythm**	HENRI MATISSE	Finding Rhythm
Unit 3 **Harmony**	JOHN WILLIAM WATERHOUSE	Art as a Political Statement
Unit 4 **Emphasis**	JOHANNES VERMEER	5 Steps to Make Your Own Political Art
Unit 5 **Proportion**	ALBRECHT DÜRER	The Mind of the Artist
Unit 6 **Movement**	SALVADOR DALI	Going into the Subconscious Mind
Unit 7 **Variety**	WINSOR MCCAY	Variety in Pop Art as Repetition

KEY VOCABULARY

expressionist, pastel, print, soul painting, nihilist

cut-out collage, expressive, Fauvist movement, mood, technique

canvas, classical, painter, Pre-Raphaelite, retrospective

Art dealer, domestic scenes, Dutch Golden Age, museum, private collection

draughtsman, oil painter, watercolors, wood cut, wood blocks

exhibition, draftsman, cubism, medium (media), surrealist

advertising, art movement, comic strip, commercial printing, pop art

UNIT	FEATURED ARTIST	CRITICAL THINKING
Unit 8 **Line**	PABLO PICASSO	Conveying Emotion with Line
Unit 9 **Color**	VINCENT VAN GOGH	Color and Psychology
Unit 10 **Form**	LEONARDO DA VINCI	Guess the Famous Painter
Unit 11 **Space**	HIERONYMOUS BOSCH	Imagining the Grotesque in Art
Unit 12 **Value**	MICHELANGELO CARAVAG-GIO	Cameos of the Artist
Unit 13 **Shape**	TAMARA DE LEMPICKA	Locating Dominate Compositional Shapes
Unit 14 **Texture**	GEORGES SEURAT	Trompe-l'œil

KEY VOCABULARY

abstraction, avant garde, color theory, sculpture, symbolism

billboard, conceptual artist, collaborated, studio, visionary art

apprentice, commissioned, patron, Renaissance man, smufato

Early Netherlandish, Flemish style, grotesque, impasto, triptych

Baroque, chiaroscuro, Mannerism, Naturalism, pupil

Art deco, commission, Neo classical, self-portrait, still life

divisionism, modern art, monochrome, pointillism, Post impressionist

Juan Gris, Playing Card and Glass of Beer 1913

Table of contents

Edvard Munch, Anxiety 1894

BALANCE

The sense of stability achieved through implied weight of an object. There are three different types of balance: symmetrical, asymmetrical, and radial.

BALANCE

MUSINGS

1. What is anxiety?

2. What is the meaning of a composition in art?

3. How does the composition by Munch make you feel? Why?

GLOSSARY

expressionist artists who express the meaning of emotional experience rather than physical reality; it developed as an avant-garde style before the First World War

pastel a kind of dried paste made of pigments ground with chalk and compounded with gum water

print a design or pattern made by engraving on a plate or block

nihilist a person who is extremely skeptical (having an attitude of doubt) about all things

soul painting painting your own emotional or psychological state

FILL IN THE BLANK WITH THE CORRECT VOCABULARY WORD

1. When on the date, Jeffery realized he had met a _____ because she questioned everything that he said.

2. During the doctor's visit, the counselor asked the sad boy to do a _____ .

3. The grandmother yelled at the child because she put _____ into the carpet.

4. The _____ threw paint onto the canvas after a day of crying and screaming to release his emotions.

5. Many of the _____ sold at the art festival.

READING COMPREHENSION

1. Where was Edvard Munch born?

2. Why did Munch have a troubled childhood?

3. What was Munch studying before he entered art school?

4. What did Hans Jæger influence Munch to become?

5. What painting is Munch most famously known for? How many times was it created in pastel and paint?

Edvard Munch

Featured Artist

Edvard Munch was a Norwegian, **expressionist**, who was born in 1863 and died in 1944. He had a troubled childhood because of sickness and the fear that he would get the mental illness that other family members had. He developed his artistic style while he was attending the Royal School of Art and Design. Before he attended the art school, he was studying engineering. Studying engineering turned out not to be a good fit for Edvard Munch. At the art school, Munch met a man named Hans Jæger. Hans was a **nihilist** and he influenced Munch to become a nihilist as well. He also encouraged Munch to do **"soul painting"**. As can be seen, Hans had a lot to do with helping Munch become the artist that he became.

Munch is most famously known for the painting, The Scream. The painting was sold at auction in 2012. It sold for the fourth largest amount of any painting ever to be auctioned off. The painting was sold for about 120 million dollars at Sotheby's auction house. Between the years 1893 and 1910, Munch, created the image The Scream twice in **pastel** and twice in **paint**. He also created many prints. Despite the harsh upbringing and judgment from an unsupportive father, who considered painters to be part of an "unholy trade", it is clear that Munch has forever changed the world of art.

The 3 Types of balance

GLOSSARY	
asymmetrical	when different types of elements create a visual imbalance
radial	the distribution of elements around a central point in all directions
symmetrical	when one image is mirrored on the other side to repeat itself

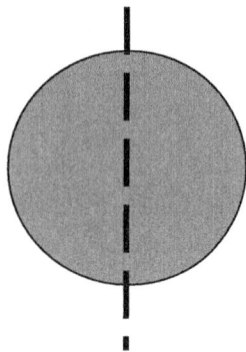

symmetrical

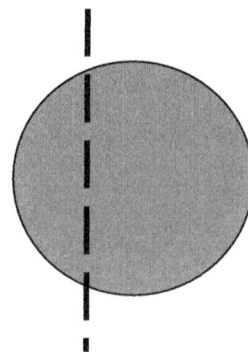

asymmetrical

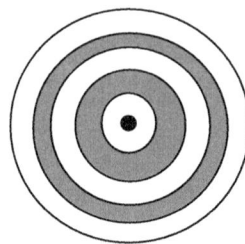

radial

Thangka of Manjuvajra artist unknown year unknown

James Whistler, Whistler's Mother 1871

Rene Magritte, Son of Man 1946©

Match the composition to the type of balance it has and explain why

1. The mandala painting

2. Whistler's Mother

3. Son of Man

GLOSSARY

aesthetic	relating to or characterized by a concern with beauty or good taste (adjective); a particular taste or approach to the visual qualities of an object (noun)
background	the area of an artwork that appears farthest away from the viewer; also, the area against which a figure or scene is placed
brushstroke	a mark made by a paintbrush drawn across a surface
composition	the arrangement of the individual elements within a work of art so as to form a unified whole
figure	a representation of a human or animal form in a work of art
foreground	the area of an image—usually a photograph, drawing, or painting—that appears closest to the viewer
scene	a setting for or a part of a story or narrative
style	a distinctive or characteristic manner of expression
subject matter	the visual or narrative focus of a work of art
tension	the quality of a work of art that creates some sense of uneasiness in the viewer because something about the balance of the composition is off.

FILL IN THE BLANK WITH THE CORRECT VOCABULARY WORD

1. The use of _____ in the painting made the viewers feel uneasy.

2. In the _____ of paintings, are items closest to the viewer.

3. The arms of the _____ were made with long, black lines.

4. To see the _____ of the painting more clearly, the art curator used a magnifying glass.

5. Madonna with child was a common _____ of Renaissance artwork.

6. The _____ of the painting was an old, French café.

7. The _____ of the painting was successful because of the balance.

8. The artist was having trouble selling his paintings, so he changed his painting _____ to appeal to more customers.

9. The still life painting was considered to be _____ (beautiful).

10. There is a mountain behind the lake in the _____ of the painting.

PHIL HALE: TENSION IN ART

Phil Hale: Tension In Art

13,722 views • Mar 17, 2016

👍 471 👎 2 ↪ SHARE ≡+ SAVE ...

Creating Tension In Art

1. Crop

2. Stretch/Skew

3. Imbalance

4. Twist

5. Strain/Pull

6. Unease (feeling)

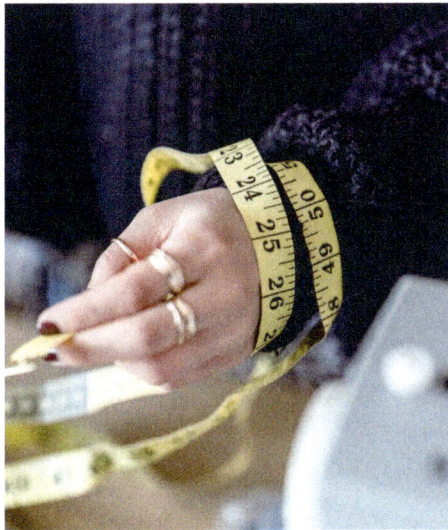

A

B

C

D

E

F

The Ambassadors, Hans Holbein the Younger 1533

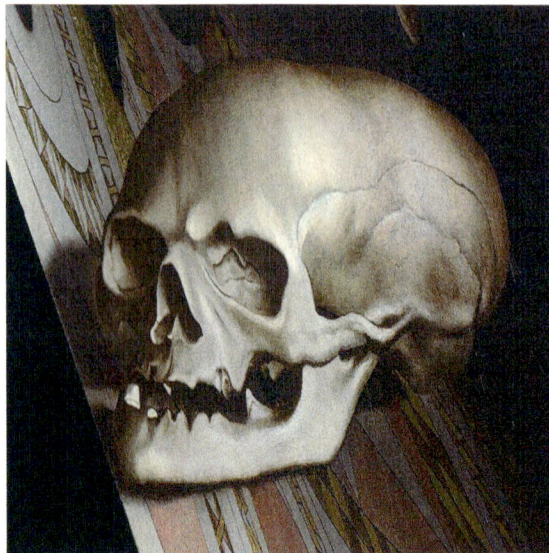

Detail The Ambassadors, Hans Holbein the Younger 1533

Paul Cézanne, Still Life with a Skull 1895-1900

DISCUSSION

1. Why do you think that Hans Holbein the Younger skewed the skull in the Ambassadors' painting?

2. Why does the above painting by Cézanne have tension in it?

3. How could you change the paintings to create more tension in them?

4. Why do you think that using tension is useful for comic book art?

THE FOCAL POINT

What is a focal point in a composition?

A focal point in a composition is the **main** area in the composition that the viewer's eye is drawn to. The focal point is a typical characteristic of classic art, however, abstract art sometimes has compositions where the focal point was deliberately not included in the composition.

METHODS FOR CREATING FOCAL POINTS

1. UNIQUENESS	The introduction of an object or element which is unusual to the scene of the composition creates uniqueness because the object will stand out.
2. CONVERGENCE	The use of implied lines which direct the viewer's eyes to a specific object or element.
3. SEPERATION	An object or element which is isolated from the other elements in the composition creates a focal point.
4. PLACEMENT	When objects are placed in the center or near the center of the picture plane in a composition, a focal point is created.
5. CONTRAST	Differences create focal points, such as color, value, texture, shape, and form.

Leonardo da Vinci, The Last Supper 15th Century

Hilda Koe, Goblin Market 1895

Martin Heade, Blue Morpho Butterfly 1865

John Sergeant, Mrs. Huth Jackson 1907

Arthur Rackman, Alice in Wonderland 1907

DISCUSSION

1. What is the type of focal point used in each painting? Why?

Edvard Munch, The Scream 1910

1. What type of balance does the composition have? Why?

2. What is something in the painting that you find aesthetic, why? What about unaesthetic, why?

3. Talk about the figure or figures.

4. What is the focal point of the painting? Why?

5. What is in the foreground of the painting?

6. What is something in the background of the painting?

Viktor Olivia, The Absinthe Drinker 1901

DIALOGUE BUILDING

The painting has a(an) _____ type of balance.

Something in the painting that I find aesthetic /unaesthetic is the...

In the painting on the left/right, the figure(s) is/are..

The focal point in the painting on the left/right is...

The foreground/background in the painting on the left/right has...

Edvard Munch, Death Struggle 1915

1. What type of balance does the composition have? Why?

2. What is something in the painting that you find aesthetic, why? What about unaesthetic, why?

3. Talk about the figure or figures.

4. What is the focal point of the painting? Why?

5. What is in the foreground of the painting?

6. What is something in the background of the painting?

Hieronymus Bosch, Christ Crowned with Thorns 1479-1516

DIALOGUE BUILDING

The painting has a(an) _____ type of balance.

Something in the painting that I find aesthetic /unaesthetic is the...

In the painting on the left/right, the figure(s) is/are..

The focal point in the painting on the left/right is...

The foreground/background in the painting on the left/right has...

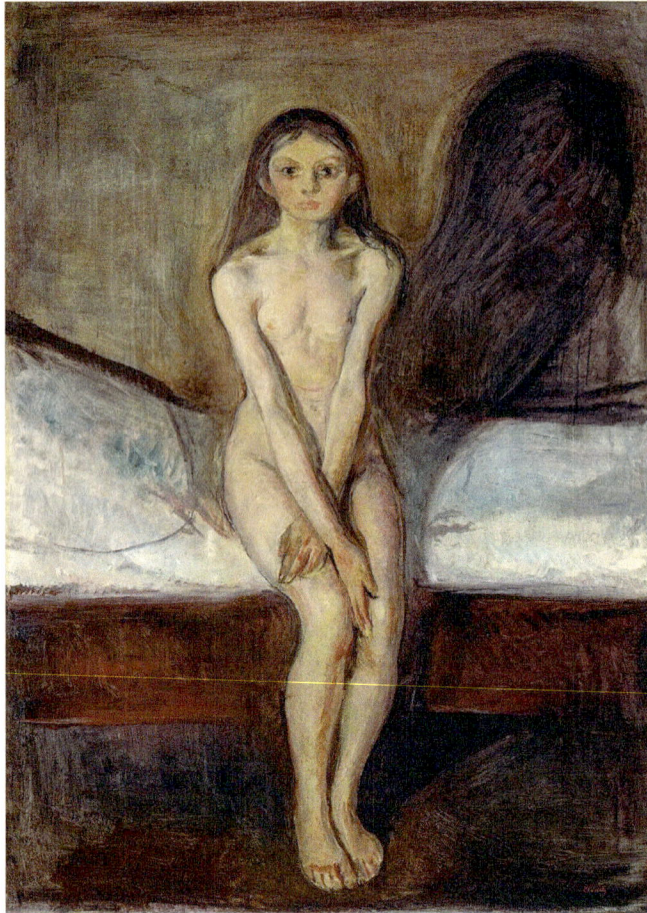

Edvard Munch, Puberty 1894-1895

1. What is the scene (setting) in the painting?

2. What is in the background in the painting?

3. What is the subject matter of the painting?

4. Is there tension in the painting? Yes or no and why or why not?

5. What do you and don't you like about the style of the painting?

Robert Delaunay, Portuguese Woman 1916

DIALOGUE BUILDING

The painting on the left/right is a scene of...

The background in the painting on the left/right has...

The subject matter in the painting on the left/right is...

There is tension in the painting on the left/right because...
There is not tension in the painting on the left/right because...

I like the style because... I do not like the style because...

EDVARD MUNCH: THE LIFE OF AN ARTIST

ANSWER THE LISTENING COMPREHENSION QUESTIONS

1. Where was Munch born?

2. What did Munch's sister and mother die from?

3. What was the name of Munch's sister with the mental health issues?

4. Why did Munch quit his engineering studies?

5. What year was Munch's first exhibition?

6. How long did Munch's relationship with Millie Thaulow last?

7. Which color combinations did the speaker claim have more expressive power?

8. The death of Munch's father put him into a state of depression and what else?

9. What's the name of Munch's most famous series of paintings?

10. What is the name of Munch's most famous painting? What year was it painted in?

11. Whose death does the speaker claim the, By the Death Bed, painting was inspired by?

12. Why did Munch decide to always wear gloves in public?

13. How much was Munch paid for the work done at the Freia chocolate factory?

14. Why did painting become more difficult for Munch in the 1930s?

15. What did Munch do a series of before he died? Why do you think that this was done?

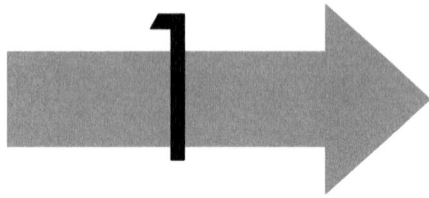

1 → Research examples of artwork: drawings, paintings, photography, etc., that show effective use of balance (asymmetry, radial, and symmetry) in the composition.

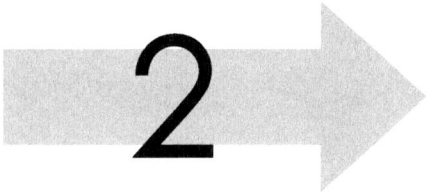

2 → Explain your reasons for why they fit the example of balance (*asymmetry, radial, and symmetry*)

3 → Identify the artists and date of each piece.

4 → Further Analysis: Use *background, foreground, subject matter, tension, focal point, scene,* etc., to add more detail to the analyses

BACK TO BALANCE

ANSWER THE FOLLOWING QUESTIONS

1. What are your sources, for example, websites that you used to locate the work? Cite each different source separately.

2. Why does each of the 3 images have the type of balance that it has? Explain your reasons thoroughly.

3. Identify the titles of the artwork, the dates of the artwork, and the artists' names.

4. Now that you have identified each piece, it's time to talk about the artwork in greater detail. Use the vocabulary terms from page 30 to add 2-3 additional sentences to your analysis of each of the artworks.

5. Share your findings with a partner. Get some feedback on your choices and whether or not your partner agrees with your opinion on if the different pieces of artwork are good examples of the three different types of balance.

Henri Matisse, The Dance 2 1910

RHYTHYM

A continual flow or sense of movement created by a pattern or repetition of visual units. It helps to achieve harmony in a composition.

RHYTHM 2

"Creativity takes courage."
-Henri Matisse

MUSINGS

1 Rhythm is a term that applies to music as well as the principles of art. Why do you think this is?

2 Can you listen to music while you also do other tasks? Yes or no, why or why not?

3 Can music influence creativity? Yes or no and why or why not?

GLOSSARY

cut-out collages	works of art created by cutting shapes out of paper or other materials and arranging them in a composition
expressive	full of emotion of feeling
Fauvist movement	a group of early 20th-century artists who emphasized the use of vivid, non-naturalistic colors
mood	the emotional atmosphere of a piece of art
technique	the method or process used to create a work of art, which can include tools, materials, and skills

FILL IN THE BLANK WITH THE CORRECT VOCABULARY WORD

1. An _____ artwork conveys strong emotion through expressive techniques.

2. In art, _____ refers to the feeling a work evokes in the viewer.

3. The _____ emphasized bright colors and stylized forms.

4. In a _____, the artist cuts and arranges shapes from colored paper or other materials.

5. A _____ is a specific way of working with materials and tools to create art.

READING COMPREHENSION

1. What was Henri Matisse's signature style as an artist?

2. What was the Fauvist movement, and how did Matisse contribute to it?

3. What artistic techniques did Matisse experiment with throughout his career?

4. In addition to his contributions to the world of art, what philanthropic efforts was Matisse known for?

5. When did Henri Matisse pass away, and what is his legacy in the art world today?

Henri Matisse

Featured Artist

Henri Matisse was a French artist known for his bold use of color, innovative **techniques**, and diverse range of styles. Born in 1869 in the town of Le Cateau-Cambrésis, Matisse initially pursued a career in law before turning to art. He studied at various academies in Paris and later moved to the south of France, where he began to develop his signature style. Matisse was a leading figure in the **Fauvist** movement, which emerged in the early 20th century and emphasized the use of vivid, non-naturalistic colors. His paintings from this period, such as "Woman with a Hat" (1905), featured bold brushstrokes and strong, contrasting colors that were considered shocking and revolutionary at the time.

Throughout his career, Matisse continued to experiment with different styles and techniques, producing a wide variety of works that ranged from paintings and drawings to **cut-out collages** and sculpture. He was particularly interested in exploring the **expressive** potential of color, and often used it to convey emotion and **mood** in his works. In addition to his contributions to the world of art, Matisse was also known for his philanthropic efforts, including the creation of a foundation to support young artists. He continued to work and create until his death in 1954, leaving behind a legacy of innovation, creativity, and beauty in his art.

The 5 Types of rhythm

GLOSSARY	
alternating	an artwork that contains a repetition of two or more components that are used interchangeably. Some alternating rhythm examples include alternating light and dark colors or placing various shapes and/or colors in a repeating pattern.
flowing	an artwork that contains curved or circular elements that give the art movement.
progressive	progressive rhythm describes an artwork that contains repeating elements in a pattern that change either in size or color as they repeat.
random	random rhythm describes an artwork that contains repeating elements without a specified order or arrangement.
regular	regular rhythm describes an artwork that contains repeating elements with a specified order or arrangement that can be measured.

Match the composition to the type of rhythm it has and explain why

1. New Order 2 2019

2. Endless Rhythm Robert Delaunay 1934

3. Farbtafel Paul Klee 1930

4. Broadway Boogie Woogie Piet Mondrian 1942-1943

5. The Great Wave of Kanaga Katsushika Hokusai 1829-1833

Katsushika Hokusai, The Great Wave of Kanaga 1829-1833

Paul Klee, Farbtafel 1930

Allyson Grey, New Order 2 2019

Robert Delaunay, Endless Rhythm 1934

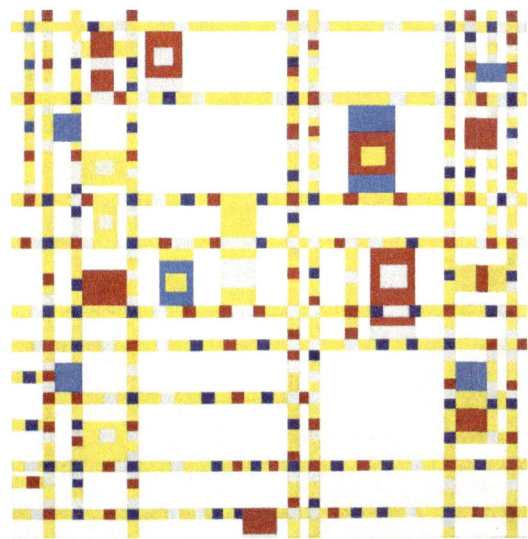

Piet Mondrian, Broadway Boogie Woogie 1942-1943

Henri Matisse, Women with a Red Umbrella Seated 1919-1921

1. Which painting(s) has alternating rhythm, why?

2. Which painting(s) has flowing rhythm, why?

3. Which painting(s) has progressive rhythm? Why?

4. Which painting(s) has random rhythm? Why?

5. Which painting(s) has regular rhythm? Why

Henri Matisse, Odalisq 1920-1921

DIALOGUE BUILDING

The painting(s) which has alternating rhythm is...because...
- Both of the paintings, have...
- Neither of the paintings, have...
- The painting on the left/right has...

The painting(s) which has flowing rhythm is...because...

The painting(s) which has progressive rhythm is...because...

The painting(s) which has random rhythm is...because...

The painting(s) which has regular rhythm is...because...

ANALYZE THE ARTWORK

1. What is in the **foreground** of the painting?

2. What is in the **background** of the painting?

3. What is the **focal point** of the painting?

4. What **focal point method** was used?

5. What is the **scene** in the painting of?

6. What type of **balance** does the painting have? Why?

7. Why is there **tension** in the painting? How is it created?

8. What type of **rhythm** does the painting have? Why?

9. What is your opinion of this **style** of painting?

DIALOGUE BUILDING

The foreground/background of the painting has...

The focal point of the painting is the...
The focal point method used in the painting is...because...

The scene in the painting is of...

The balance in the painting is...because...

The tension in the painting is used to. .. Tension is created by...

The type of rhythm that the painting has is...because...

I think that the style of the painting is...because...

Henri Matisse, *Interior with a Violin* 1918

Finding Rhythm
Matching music genres to artwork

LISTEN TO EACH SONG AND DECIDE HOW YOU COULD USE THE FIVE TYPES OF RHYTHM TO SHOW HOW THE MUSIC LOOKS AS ARTWORK

Describe your vision for each genre of music in at least 3 sentences for each song

1.   Genre?
        What type of rhythm would you use to represent this
        sound? Why?

2.   Genre?
        What type of rhythm would you use to represent this
        sound? Why?

3.   Genre?
        What type of rhythm would you use to represent this
        sound? Why?

4.   Genre?
        What type of rhythm would you use to represent this
        sound? Why?

5.   Pick 4 different genres of music that are not listed and de-
        scribe what types of rhythm you would use to represent
        those sounds and explain why.

6.   Add additional songs here, and which type of rhythm they
        represent.

John William Waterhouse, Nymphs Finding the Head of Orpheus 1900

HARMONY

The quality of how the visual elements are working together in a composition. It is achieved when all elements have unity and cohesion, giving a sense of completion to an artwork. This does not mean that all elements have to be the same, but they must relate to each other in a purposeful way. Harmony can be achieved through the use of analogous colors on the color wheel, and by using similar shapes and forms.

HARMONY 3

MUSINGS

1. Outside of the art world, what does the word harmony mean?

2. What colors in your culture are associated with sadness, death, happiness?

3. Why do you think that people like to associate different colors with feelings or ideas?

GLOSSARY

canvas	a surface you paint on that is often made from tightly stretched, un-bleached cloth or a closely woven fabric
classical	art produced by ancient Greek and Roman civilizations, covers a time period of roughly ten centuries
painter	an artist who paints pictures
Pre–Raphaelite	a member of a group of English 19th-century artists, who sought to copy the simplicity and sincerity of the work of Italian artists from before the time of Raphael
retrospective	an art exhibit that covers an artist's entire career is called a retrospective because it looks back at the work the artist has produced over many years

FILL IN THE BLANK WITH THE CORRECT VOCABULARY WORD

1. Sadly, the elderly artist died right before his _____ exhibit.

2. The new _____ that Patricia bought was very expensive.

3. The child said that he wants to be a _____ when he grows up.

4. The English artist loved Italian art, so, he studied the _____ artists from his country to learn more.

5. _____ art focuses on making the human body appear very realistic.

READING COMPREHENSION

1. When was John William Waterhouse born?

2. What was the first style that Waterhouse painted in?

3. What style of art did a group of artists create?

4. Why did the Pre-Raphaelite Brotherhood rebel against the academy?

5. Who are the two famous subjects that Waterhouse painted?

John William Waterhouse

Featured Artist

John William Waterhouse does not have an exact birth date on any known record available, but, he was baptized on April 6th 1849, and he died on February 10th 1917. He was an English **painter**, who first worked in the **classical** style and then moved on to the **Pre-Raphaelite** style. Academic art is the style that was being taught in art institutions. In response to that, the Pre-Raphaelite style is the style that was created by a group of artists in 1848. The group of young artists, who called themselves the pre-Raphaelite Brotherhood, consisted of Dante Gabriel Rossetti, William Michael Rossetti, Thomas Woolner, William Holman Hunt, Frederic George Stephens, James Collinson, and John Everett Millais. These artists rebelled against the way that they were being instructed at the Royal Academy of Art in London. They thought that the training was boring and limiting. They found that they were not able to truly express themselves in the artistic process due to the unimaginative style. The style that the artists agreed on that allowed them to properly express themselves was the style of art that was created in Italy, before the time of the artist named Raphael. This is why their style of art is called Pre-Raphaelite.

Waterhouse created many large **canvas** works that depicted subjects such as daily life, and the mythology of ancient Greece. Many art galleries currently have work of Waterhouse on exhibit. The Royal Academy of Art, where Waterhouse studied from 1871, held a **retrospective** exhibit of his artwork in 2009. One of Waterhouse's best known subjects is the Lady of Shallot. The Lady of Shallot is from the popular poem about a woman who dies mysteriously of cancer after looking directly at the man that she admired. He painted three different versions of this painting, in 1888, 1894, and 1916. Another famous painting of Waterhouse is Ophelia, which is another character from a famous work of literature.

ANALOGOUS COLORS CREATE HARMONY

Analogous color schemes can create harmonious paintings.

To find analogous colors, pick any color on the color wheel and then chose the next 3-4 colors next to it to the right or the left of the chosen color.

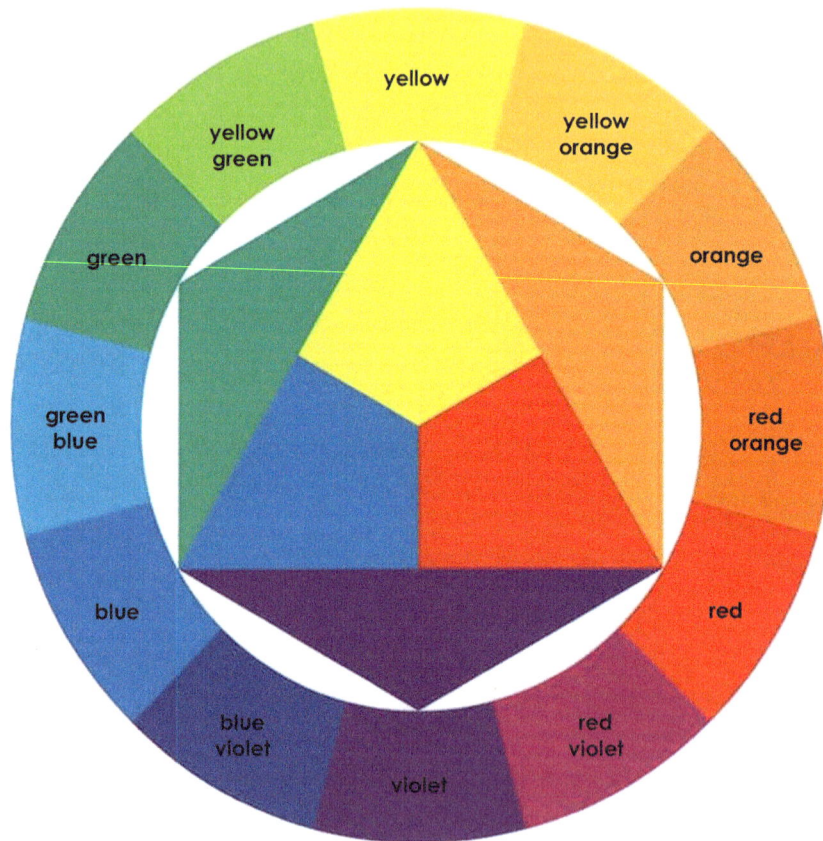

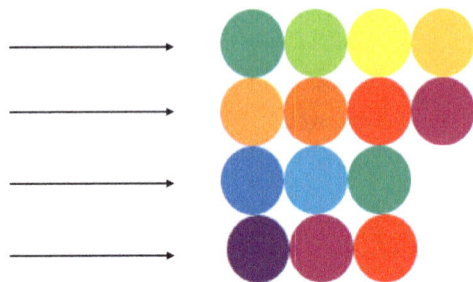

The Color Wheel

A color wheel shows how colors are related. On a color wheel, each secondary color is between the primary colors that are used to make it.

high key analogous colors	colors on the high end of the value scale
mid key analogous colors	colors in the middle of the value scale
low key analogous colors	colors on the low end of the value scale

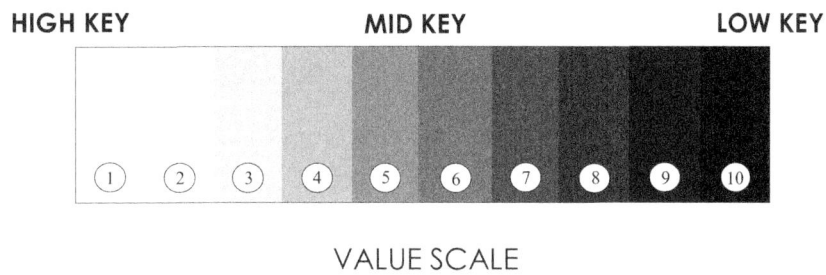

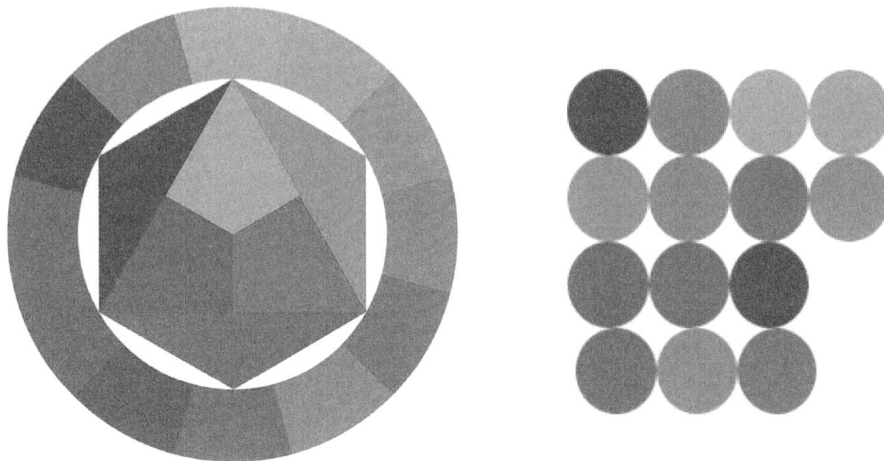

HIGH KEY   MID KEY   LOW KEY

① ② ③ ④ ⑤ ⑥ ⑦ ⑧ ⑨ ⑩

VALUE SCALE

DISCUSSION

1. Which analogous colors are high key?

2. Which analogous colors are mid key?

3. Which analogous colors are low key?

PAINTINGS WITH ANALOGOUS COLORS
LOW KEY, MID KEY, HIGH KEY

Claude Monet, Morning on the Seine 1897

Emile Claus, Summer 1893

Rembrandt van Rijn, Philosopher in Meditation 1623

John Henry Fuseli, The Shepherd's Dream 1793

DISCUSSION

1. Which painting shows predominately low key analogous colors?

2. Which painting shows predominately mid key analogous colors?

3. Which painting shows predominately high key analogous colors?

4. What is the key of the predominately analogous colors in the painting above?

5. What effect does this key have on the feeling that the painting gives the viewer? Why?

SIMILAR SHAPES CREATE HARMONY

Paul Klee, Castles and Sun 1928

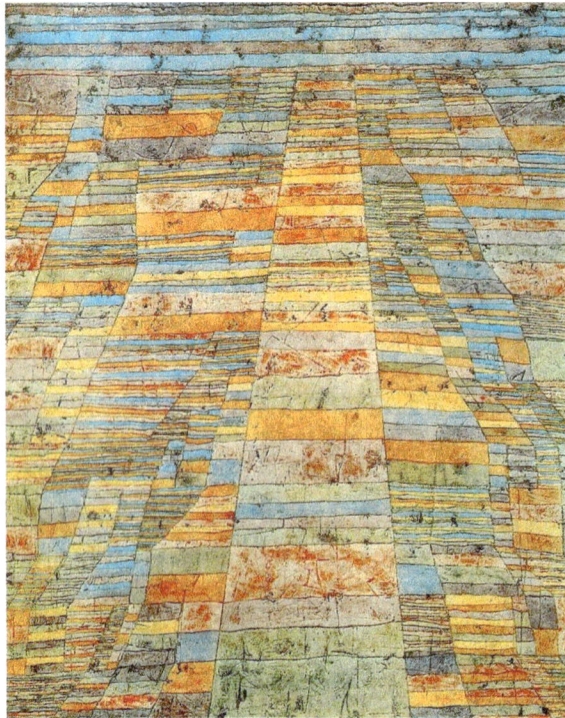

Paul Klee, Highways and Byways 1929

John William Waterhouse Flora and the Zephyrs 1898

John William Waterhouse, Sleep and His Half Brother Death 1874

1. Which shapes are creating harmony in the Flora and the Zephyrs painting? How?

2. Which shapes are creating harmony in the Sleep and His Half Brother death painting? How?

John William Waterhouse, Circe Invidiosa 1891

John William Waterhouse, Destiny 1900

1. Comment on the harmony in regards to analogous colors in the Circe Invidiosa painting.

2. Comment on the harmony in regards to shape in the Circe Invidiosa painting.

3. Comment on the harmony in regards to analogous colors in the Destiny painting.

4. Comment on the harmony in regards to shape in the Destiny painting.

1. What is in the **foreground** of the painting?

2. What is in the **background** of the painting?

3. What is the **focal point** of the painting?

4. What **focal point method** was used?

5. What is the **scene** in the painting of?

6. What type of **balance** does the painting have? Why?

7. Why is there **tension** in the painting? How is it created?

8. What type of **rhythm** does the painting have? Why?

9. What is your opinion of this **style** of painting?

10. Which part of the color wheel are the analogous colors on?

11. How is **harmony** represented with shapes?

12. Are the colors mainly **high key**, **mid key** or **low key**?

John William Waterhouse, Lamia 1905

THE PRE-RAPHAELITE BROTHERHOOD

John Everet Millias, detail Isabella 1848

THE BROTHERHOOD'S EARLY DOCTRINE

1. To have genuine ideas to express

2. To study nature attentively, so as to know how to express it

3. To sympathize with what is direct and serious and heart-felt in previous art, to the exclusion of what is conventional and self-parodying and learned by rote

4. Most indispensable of all, to produce thoroughly good pictures and statues

John Everet Millias, Isabella 1848

DISCUSSION

1. Is it important that art expresses genuine/true ideas? Yes or no and why or why not?

2. Why do you think that the second doctrine was important to the brotherhood?

3. Why is the third doctrine important for creators of art?

4. What is your opinion of the fourth doctrine? Do you agree with it? Why or why not?

5. Which of the statements do you resonate with (feel connected to) the most? Why?

6. The Pre-Raphaelite Brotherhood started out as a secret society. Why do you think that was?

7. Why do you think that the movement was successful?

LADY OF SHALOTT ART ANALYSIS
(VIDEO ESSAY)

ANSWER THE LISTENING COMPREHENSION QUESTIONS

1. Why is the face of the Lady of Shallot forlorn?

2. What was the painting based on?

3. What was the Lady of Shallot forced to do in her home?

4. Who does she fall in love with through the mirror?

5. What happens after she turns from her work?

6. What is symbolic of her life ebbing away?

7. What is symbolic of a fallen woman?

8. Go to nature rejecting _____, selecting _____, and scorning _____.

9. What does her life lack?

10. The Pre-Raphaelites felt themselves compelled to go to what?

Hunt, the Awakening Conscience

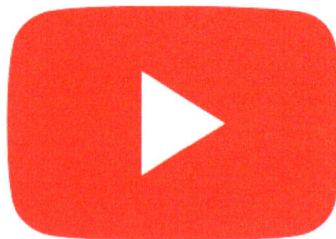

ART AS A POLITICAL STATEMENT

The Pre-Raphaelite Brotherhood had a political message that they wanted to get across. They wanted to revolutionize British art. They did not relate to the style of art that was popular at the time because it was commercialized and conventional.

They felt that the artwork that they were taught didn't help them show the intimacy, the beauty, and the intensity of the everyday life that was around them. For content to paint, the artists often looked to literature that spoke of fantastical themes such as mythological creatures, heroes, and terrible villains.

They did a subtle protest by signing their paintings with the Brotherhood's initials and coming up with a doctrine that stated what they thought that art should be. They challenged the existing system and painted subjects in new ways, and with new painting techniques to deliver a brand new message.

RESEARCH QUESTIONS

1. What was happening in the society during the time of the Pre-Raphaelite Brotherhood? Why do you think this?

2. How can a change in the style of art influence culture?

3. Can you think of a style of art that has changed culture? What is it and how did it change the culture?

4. What is the meaning of awakening conscience?

5. What does the awakening conscience have to do with culture?

5. What is a muse and what is their purpose in art?

7. What role did the bright, and vibrant color palette have to do with this movement?

Johannes Vermeer, Girl with the Pearl Earring 1665

EMPHASIS

When one element of an artwork stands out more than another. This creates a sense of importance and is intentionally used to communicate a message or feeling. Emphasis creates variety in your artwork.

EMPHASIS 4

"I never paint dreams or nightmares, I paint my own reality."
-Johannes Vermeer

MUSINGS

1. What is censorship?

2. What are your thoughts on the censorship of artwork? Why is it good or bad for a society?

3. Some artwork is created to raise awareness about a situation. Who is an artist that you know that creates that sort of artwork?

GLOSSARY

art dealer	A person or business that buys and sells works of art, usually for profit.
domestic scenes	Scenes of everyday life in the home, such as family gatherings, cooking, or other household activities.
Dutch Golden Age	A period of economic, cultural, and artistic growth in the Netherlands during the 17th century.
museum	Institutions that collect, preserve, and display works of art and other cultural artifacts for public viewing.
private collection	Personal collections of art owned by individuals or organizations, often not on public display.

FILL IN THE BLANK WITH THE CORRECT VOCABULARY WORD

1. The _____ was a period in Dutch art history known for its realistic depictions of everyday life, landscapes, and still lifes.

2. A _____ is a collection of art owned by a private individual or organization, and not open to public viewing.

3. _____ depict everyday life, often within a household or family setting.

4. A _____ is a public institution that collects and displays art for public viewing.

5. An _____ buys and sells art, often for profit.

READING COMPREHENSION

1. Who was Johannes Vermeer?

2. What is Vermeer's style of painting known for?

3. What were some of the subjects Vermeer often painted?

4. Was Vermeer famous during his lifetime?

5. What influence did Vermeer have on Dutch painting?

Johannes Vermeer

Featured Artist

Johannes Vermeer was a Dutch painter who lived from 1632 to 1675. He was born in Delft, a city in the Netherlands, and spent his entire life there. Vermeer was not widely recognized during his lifetime and his works were largely forgotten until the 19th century. Vermeer's early life is not well-documented, but it is known that he came from a middle-class family and that his father was an **art dealer**. Vermeer likely received some training as a painter from his father, but the extent of his formal education is not clear. Vermeer's paintings are admired for their use of light and color, which create a sense of intimacy and realism. He was particularly interested in the effects of light on surfaces, such as the way that light reflects off a pearl or a piece of fabric. Vermeer also paid close attention to the details of everyday life, and his paintings often depict **domestic scenes**, such as women sewing or reading, or men playing musical instruments.

Despite the fact that Vermeer was not widely recognized during his lifetime, he was influential in the development of Dutch painting. His use of light and color was particularly important to the development of the Dutch Golden Age style of painting, which emphasized realism and naturalism. Today, Vermeer is considered one of the greatest painters of the **Dutch Golden Age**. His works are highly prized and are held in major **museums** and **private collections** around the world.

The 6 Types of emphasis

1. Contrast a shape with its surroundings

2. Create a contrast of temperatures between warm and cool colors

3. Focus viewer's attention with converging lines (two or more lines that get closer and closer towards the end)

4. Isolate the object that needs to be emphasized

5. Increase an objects intensity/saturation of color by using a more pure color

6. Use a lighter or darker value

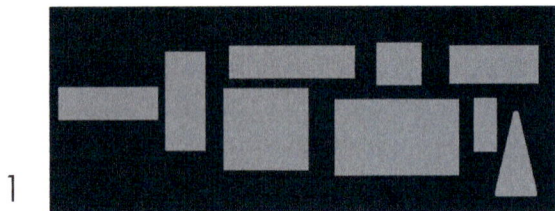

1

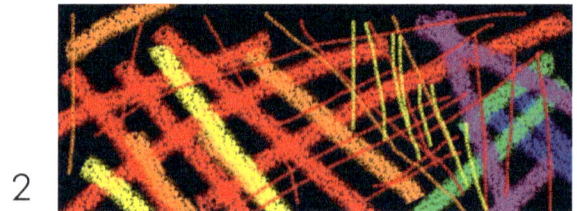

2

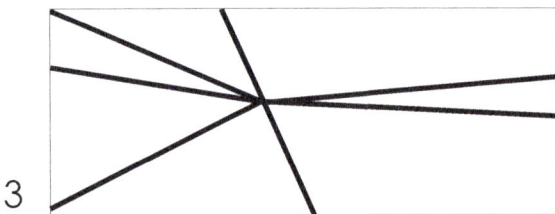

3

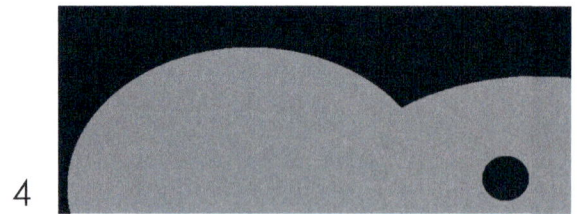

4

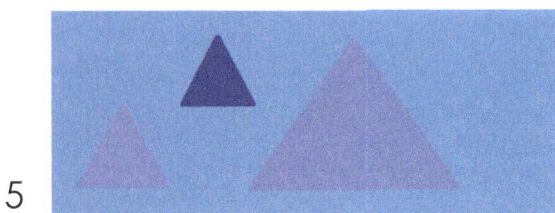

5

6

Match the composition to the type of emphasis it has and explain why

Claude Monet, Impression Sunrise 1872

Henry Fuseli Titania, Bottom and the Fairies 1794

Jacques Louis David, The Death of Socrates 1787

Joseph Turner, Hannibal and His Army Crossing the Alps 1812

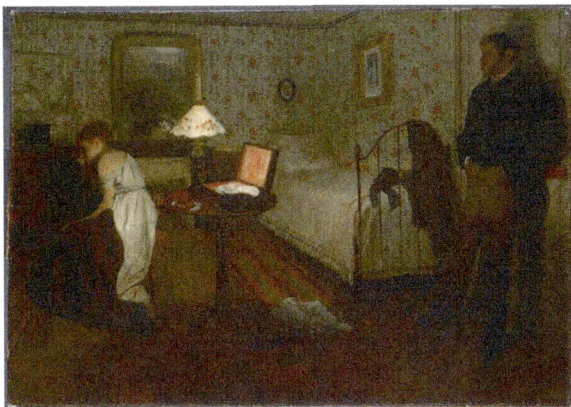
Edgar Degas, Interior 1868-1869

John Singer Sergeant, Parisian Beggar Girl 1880

Johannes Vermeer, The Milkmaid 1658

1. Which type of emphasis is used? How?

2. What social commentary is being made in the image?

3. What is your opinion of the artwork?

4. How does the artwork make you feel?

DIALOGUE BUILDING

The type of emphasis that is used is... It is used by...

The social commentary that is being made is...
The social commentary has to do with...

My opinion of the artwork is...
I think that...

When I look at the image, I feel...because...

Johannes Vermeer, The Art of Painting 1666

1. Which type of emphasis is used? How?

2. What social commentary is being made in the image?

3. What is your opinion of the artwork?

4. How does the artwork make you feel?

DIALOGUE BUILDING

The type of emphasis that is used is... It is used by...

The social commentary that is being made is...
The social commentary has to do with...

My opinion of the artwork is...
I think that...

When I look at the image, I feel...because...

1. What is in the **foreground** of the painting?

2. What is in the **background** of the painting?

3. What is the **focal point** of the painting?

4. What **focal point method** was used?

5. What is the **scene** in the painting of?

6. What type of **balance** does the painting have? Why?

7. Is there **tension** in the painting? If so, how is it created?

8. What type of **rhythm** does the painting have? Why?

9. What is your opinion of this **style** of painting?

10. How is **harmony** represented with shapes or analogous colors?

11. What type of **emphasis** does this painting have? How?

12. What social commentary is being made with this painting?

13. Do you agree with the social commentary being made about this painting? Why or why not?

Johannes Vermeer, Woman Holding a Balance 1664

What is Political Art?

Political art is a form of art that engages with political and social issues, and often seeks to critique or challenge the status quo. Political art can take many different forms, including painting, sculpture, performance art, street art, and more. The goal of political art is to raise awareness about political and social issues, to encourage critical thinking and discussion, and to inspire action towards positive change.

- Draws attention to important issues
- Sparks conversation and debate
- Encourages meaningful engagement with complex issues
- Serves as a catalyst for social and political change
- Plays a crucial role in shaping society and the world
- Interconnected with social and political movements

George Grosz's "The Stützen der Gesellschaft" (1926): This painting, which translates to "The Pillars of Society," is a scathing critique of the political and social elite of Weimar Germany. The work depicts a group of wealthy and powerful figures who are shown as greedy and corrupt.

George Groszs, The Stützen der Gesellschaft 1926

CASES FOR POLITICAL ART : THE ART ASSIGNMENT : PBS DIGITAL STUDIOS

ANSWER THE MULTIPLE CHOICE QUESTIONS

1. Political art is also called?

   A. protest art   **B.** politically motivated art

   C. activist art   **D.** socially engaged art

2. Which medium did Kathe Kollwitz use to create her work?

   A. sculpture   **B.** drawing

   C. painting   **D.** printmaking

3. Which shape did Kazmir Malevich take refuge in?

   A. circle   **B.** rectangle

   C. triangle   **D.** square

4. What did Kazmir Malevich call his art style of shapes and forms?

   A. suprematism   **B.** capitalism

   C. superrealism   **D.** superiority

5. What was the name of the protest mural created by Pablo Picasso?

   A. Qwernika   **B.** Guernica

   C. Wernika   **D.** Shernija

6. How many years did Iri and Toshi Mariki paint panels about the Hiroshima bombings?

   A. 10   **B.** 22

   C. 32   **D.** 12

5 STEPS TO MAKE YOUR OWN POLITICAL ART

1 USE ICONIC IMAGERY!

2 DEVELOP A DISTINCTIVE TECHNIQUE!

3 TAP INTO THE TOPICAL!

4 MAKE YOUR ART APPROACHABLE!

5 GET YOUR ART OUT THERE!

5 Steps to Make Your Own Political Art

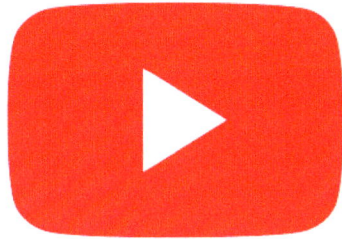

DISCUSSION

1. What is your opinion of political art?

2. Do you have a political artist whose work you like?

3. What is a past or present social issue that you would like to see made into political art? Why?

Albrecht Dürer , The Four Horsemen of the Apocalypse 1498

PROPORTION

The ratio of one art element to another; the relationship between different elements of the composition so that the scale of the artwork makes visual sense.

PROPORTION 5

"What beauty is, I know not, though it adheres to many things. If a man devotes himself to art, much evil is avoided that happens otherwise if one is idle."
-Albrecht Dürer

MUSINGS

1. Why would an artist deliberately distort proportions in their artwork?

2. What does mathematics have to do with proportion?

3. What do you know about Leonardo Da Vinci?

GLOSSARY

draughtsman   A person who draws, sketches, plans, or designs

oil painter   a painter who paints with pigments with a medium of drying oil as the binder

watercolors   artists' paint made with a water-soluble binder such as gum arabic, and thinned with water rather than oil, giving a transparent color

wood cut   the oldest form of printmaking, a relief process in which knives and other tools are used to carve a design into a wooden block

wood block   a style of relief printing in which artists use carved wooden blocks to prese designs onto textiles or paper

FILL IN THE BLANK WITH THE CORRECT VOCABULARY WORD

1. An artist who paints using oil paints is called an _____.

2. In printmaking, a design is cut into a block of wood to create a print. This process is known as _____ .

3. The block of wood used in printmaking to create a print is called a _____.

4. The type of paints are mixed with water _____.

5. A person who is skilled in drawing is known as a _____.

READING COMPREHENSION

1. What was Albrecht Dürer known for?

2. Who did Dürer apprentice under as a young artist?

3. What is notable about Dürer's woodcut print "The Four Horsemen of the Apocalypse"?

4. What is one of Dürer's most famous paintings, and what is notable about it?

5. How did Dürer use mathematical and scientific principles in his art?

Albrecht Dürer

Featured Artist

Albrecht Dürer was a German artist born in Nuremberg in 1471. He is known for his innovative work in printmaking, as well as his skill as an **oil painter**, **draughtsman**, and mathematician. Dürer also had experience with **watercolors** and engraving. Dürer's art was highly influential in the Northern Renaissance. Dürer began his artistic career as an apprentice to his father, a goldsmith, but quickly showed a talent for drawing and painting. He trained under several influential artists in his early years, including Michael Wolgemut, who was a master of **woodcut** printmaking. One of Dürer's most famous works is his woodcut print "The Four Horsemen of the Apocalypse" (1498), which depicts four horsemen representing war, pestilence, famine, and death. The print is notable for its intricate details, which were achieved through the use of multiple **woodblocks**, and its powerful composition, which makes use of strong diagonal lines and dramatic contrasts of light and dark.

In addition to his work in printmaking, Dürer was also an accomplished painter. He is known for his portraits, which were highly detailed and often featured a strong sense of psychological insight. One of his most famous paintings is "Self-Portrait" (1500), which depicts Dürer at the age of 28, looking directly at the viewer with a calm and confident gaze. Throughout his career, Dürer was also deeply interested in mathematical and scientific principles, and he used these ideas to inform his art. He was particularly interested in the golden ratio, which he used to create compositions that were both balanced and dynamic. His painting "Melencolia I" (1514) is a great example of this, featuring a complex composition that includes a number of mathematical and symbolic elements. In conclusion, Albrecht Dürer was a highly skilled and innovative artist who made significant contributions to the Northern Renaissance. His use of mathematical and scientific principles in his art continues to fascinate and inspire artists and viewers to this day.

Proportion in Nature

GLOSSARY	
Fibonacci sequence	a pattern that starts with 0 then each following number is the sum of the two before it; 0, 1, 1, 2, 3, 5, 8, 13, 21, 34, 55, 89, 144... As the numbers go higher, the ratio between the numbers gets closer to PHI; Some believe this sequence explains growth in nature. Greek sculptor Phidias is said to have used this number to determine the proportions of his sculptures
golden ratio	the irrational number Φ PHI, which is 1.61803398875; also known as the divine proportion
golden rectangle	a rectangle that has a ratio between it's sides that match PHI; a rectangle whose side lengths are successive Fibonacci numbers
golden spiral	a logarithmic spiral whose growth factor is Φ, the golden ratio; that is, a golden spiral gets wider (or further from its origin) by a factor of Φ for every quarter turn it makes
Φ PHI	the Greek letter used to indicate the golden ratio
golden section (PHI grid)	a variation on the "rule of thirds" which divides a frame into three rows and three columns of equal size creating in 1:1:1 vertically and 1:1:1 horizontally; the Phi Grid divides the frame in a similar way, but makes the middle row and middle column smaller according to the golden ratio, resulting in 1:1.618:1 vertically and 1:1.618:1 horizontally
golden triangle	the frame is divided into four triangles of two different sizes, done by drawing one diagonal from one corner to another, and then two lines from the other corners, touching the first at 90 degree angles
Vitruvian man	a mathematical study of the human form, created in the 16th century by Da Vinci. It represents the ideal proportion of the human form as understood by Greeks; indicates how the various parts of the human body compare to each other and the larger whole

Match the image to the definition

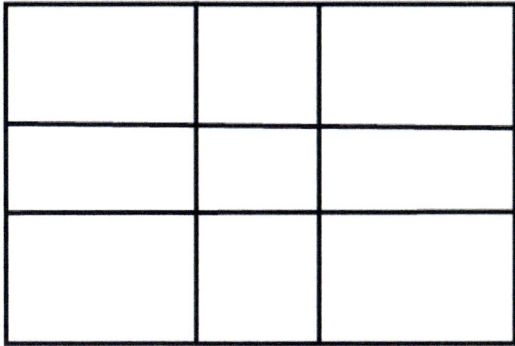

1

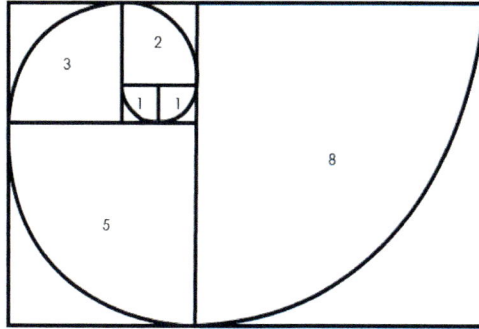

2

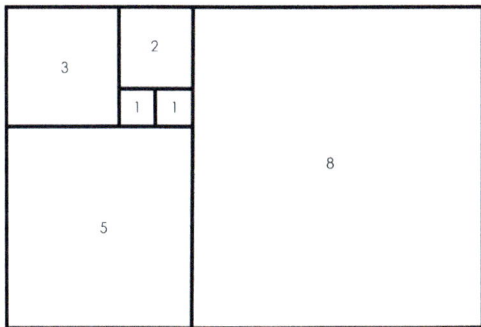

3

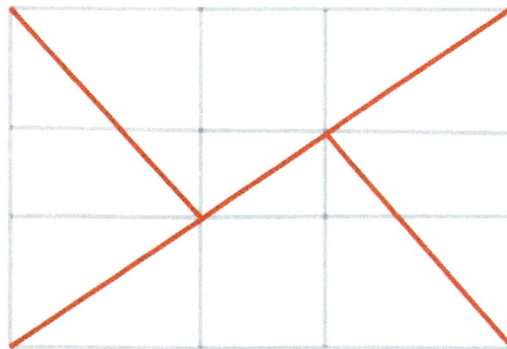

4

Φ

5

1.61803398

6

0, 1, 1, 2, 3, 5, 8, 13, 21, 34, 55,89, 144...

7

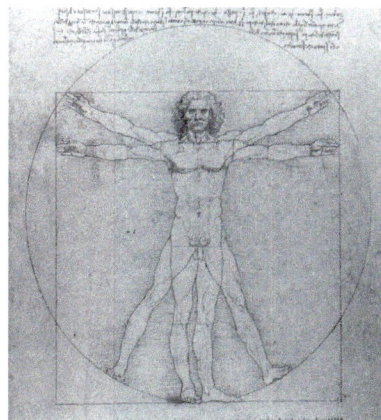

8

Match the proportion type with the paintings and explain why

Georges Seurat, Bridge at Courbevoie 1887

Frans Snyder, Dogs Fighting 1650

Sandro Botticelli, The Birth of Venus 1484–1486

THE GREEK SEARCH FOR PERFECTION

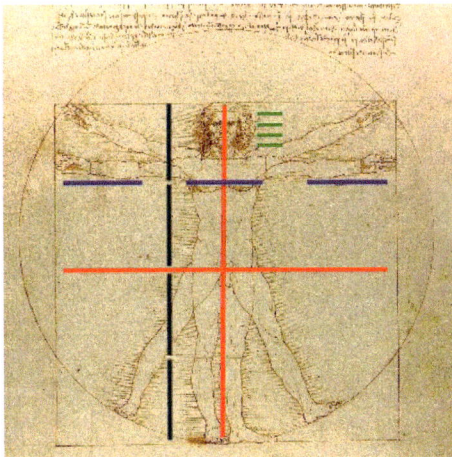

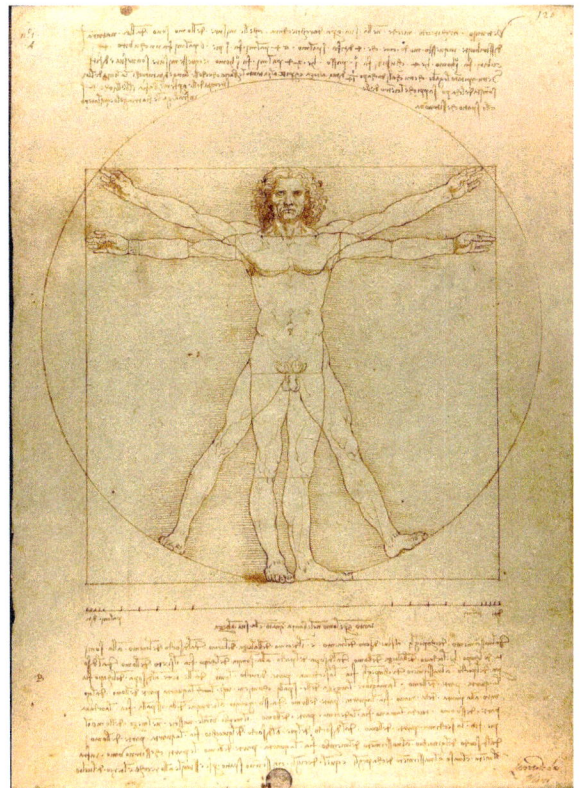

Leonardo DaVinci Vitruvian Man 1490

Height
- **head** = 1/8 total height
- **hand** = 1/10 total height
- **foot** = 1/6 total height

red
- arms outstretched, height and width are equal

black
- the knees are halfway between the genitals and the feet
- the chest is halfway between the genitals and the top of the head

blue
- the chest is the same width as a quarter of the height
- the measurement from the elbow to the fingertips is also a quarter of the height

green
- the nose is halfway between the hairline and the chin
- the lips are halfway between the nose and chin
- the eyebrows are halfway between the nose and hairline

1. What is halfway between the hairline and the chin?

2. What proportion is the head to the total height on the body?

3. What is the measurement from the elbow to the fingertips?

4. What is 1/6 the total height of the body?

5. The chest is the same width as what?

Unrealistic Proportion

Exaggerated or distorted proportions are sometimes used by artists to make a particular statement or send a certain message. The artist can create this mood by lengthening, widening, shrinking, and bending parts of the human body.

Quentin Matsys, A Grotesque Woman 1513

Parmigianino, Madonna with the Long Neck 1535-1540

El Greco, The Burial of Count Orgaz 1586-1588

Francisco De Goya, The Colossus 1808-1812

Théodore Géricault , The Raft of Medusa 1818-1819

DISCUSSION

1. What is something unrealistic or exaggerated from each of the paintings?

Albrecht Dürer , Adam and Eve 1504

1. Comment on the proportion type.

2. What message does the proportion convey?

Albrecht Dürer, Melencolia I 1514

1. Comment on the proportion type.

2. What message does the proportion convey?

Albrecht Dürer , The Great Piece of Turf 1503

1. What is in the **foreground** of the painting?

2. What is in the **background** of the painting?

3. What is the **focal point** of the painting?

4. What **focal point method** was used?

5. What is the **scene** in the painting of?

6. What type of **balance** does the painting have? Why?

7. Why is there **tension** in the painting? How is it created?

8. What type of **rhythm** does the painting have? Why?

9. What is your opinion of this **style** of painting?

10. Which side of the color wheel are the colors on?

11. How is **harmony** represented with shapes?

12. Are the colors mainly **high key**, **mid key** or **low key**? Why?

13. Comment on the **proportion**

DüRER'S WOODCUTS AND ENGRAVINGS

ANSWER THE GAP FILL QUESTIONS

1. Dürer was from _____.

2. Dürer was a great painter, but also a great _____.

3. There were several different types of _____ that were popular in the late 1400s and early 1500s.

4. And the _____ were the first and most popular.

5. One of the most important reasons was the way a woodcut is _____.

6. All of the _____ that have been printed on the page.

7. The carver, had carved away everything that is white and _____.

8. It's like a _____.

9. They help spread your name or your _____ quickly.

10. What he is able to do, later in his life is take advantage of _____ printing technique.

11. With an engraving, you work with a _____ plate.

12. Dürer was able to achieve the kind of _____ and textural nuances.

13. You can print fewer _____ than you can a woodcut.

14. It's amazing how he is able to achieve with an engraving the characteristic features of northern European _____.

15. It is quite evident that Dürer has used _____ point perspective.

What is an art critique? An art critique is a careful study of artwork to learn about its parts, what they do, and how they are related to each other. An art critique also judges the value or condition of a work of art in a thoughtful way. No two people will ever critique the same work of art in the same way, but there are basic guidelines to follow to have a meaningful and thorough art critique.

Part 1

Detailing the work

• **Gather basic information about the artwork**
Title of the work
Artist's name
When the piece was created
Where it was made
The types of media used to create the work (e.g., oil paint on canvas)
The exact size of the work

• **Describe what you see**
Discuss the subject of the work
Talk about the scale of the work
(Be sure not to use terms like, ugly, good, or bad)

• **Discuss the elements of the work** (line, shape, form, space, value, color, texture)
What do you notice about the seven elements of art ?

For example, what types of lines are used in the work? Are geometric or organic shapes used? Is there a variety of shapes or is one type of shape dominate? How is light and shading used to create form? How are depth and perspective used to show space? How is the value used (lightness and darkness)? How do the colors work together? What can you see in the texture? Is the texture smooth, or rough?

Part 2

Figuring out the work

• **Discuss the principles of the work** (balance, rhythm, harmony, emphasis, proportion, variety, movement)

For example, balance: How do the colors, shapes, and textures in the piece work together? Do they create a balanced or harmonious effect, or is the piece imbalanced in some way? How is a sense of flow shown with rhythm? How do unity and cohesion show harmony? What was emphasized in the artwork, or what is your eye drawn to first? Why were you drawn to that feature first? Do the sizes of the different elements in the work appear the way you would expect, or are they surprising? In what ways has variety been shown in the artwork? How does the work create a sense of movement? Is your eye drawn through the composition in a particular way?

- **Look for themes in the work**

How does a color scheme create a mood or meaning?

How are symbolism and religious or mythological imagery used?

How are repeating images or motifs within a work or group of works used?

<table>
<tr><td>**Part 3**</td><td></td></tr>
</table>

Explaining the meaning of the work

What do you think the artist was trying to say with the work? Why did they create the work? Try to summarize the overall meaning of the work .

- **Describe your reaction to the work**

Think about how you feel while looking at the work. What do you think is the overall mood of the work? Does it remind you of anything (ideas, experiences, other works of art)?

- **Back up your interpretation with examples**

Use examples of the principles or elements of art as examples to your interpretation of the artwork. For example, "*I think that the artwork means that… because the lines in the artwork…*"

Part 4 — Your opinion of the work

- **Decide whether you think the work is successful or not**

Do you think the work says what the artist wanted it to say?

Did the artist use their tools and techniques well?

Is the art original, or does it imitate other works?

- **Summarize why you think the work is successful or unsuccessful.**

Use specific reasons (the elements and principles of art) for your judgment

For example, "*I think that the artwork is successful because the proportions, the color, etc., …*"

DISCUSSION

1. Why are art critiques important?

2. What benefits can artists gain from art critiques?

3. In which part of the art critique would you discuss what your eye is drawn to first? Why?

4. In which part of the art critique would you discuss the place where the artwork was made? Why?

5. In which part of the art critique would you discuss your feelings about the artwork? Why?

Salvador Dali, Venus and Cupids 1925

MOVEMENT

The visual flow of your artwork. It's the path that you intend your viewer's eye to follow. You can create this by purposefully placing art elements in a way that creates this path.

MOVEMENT 6

MUSINGS

1. What is moving in the Dali painting on the left?

2. What message do you think that the artist was trying to convey with the subject matter in the painting? Why?

3. Describe the last strange dream that you can remember.

GLOSSARY

exhibition	the space in which art objects meet an audience. The exhibit is usually temporary unless it is a "permanent exhibition"
draftsman	a person employed in making mechanical drawings, as of machines, structures; etc. a person who draws sketches, plans, or designs; an artist exceptionally skilled in drawing
cubism	a movement in art that began in France in 1907 that is characterized by the use of geometric planes and shapes
medium (media)	a medium is the art technique or material that you use to express your art, such as watercolor, oil paint, gouache, ink on paper etc. Media is plural or medium
surrealist	an artist who is a believer in this avant-garde movement in art and literature which sought to release the creative potential of the unconscious mind

FILL IN THE BLANK WITH THE CORRECT VOCABULARY WORD

1. They car company hired a _____ to design new, creative bodies.

2. Because he was interested in painting dreams, he studied the _____ of the early 1900s.

3. Her favorite _____ to use for making art is colored pastels.

4. _____ is the famous style that Pablo Picasso often painted in.

5. The _____ featured artwork from the early 20th century.

READING COMPREHENSION

1. What nationality was Salvador Dali?

2. What styles first influenced Dali?

3. When did he develop his surrealist style?

4. What is the name of Dali's most famous work?

5. What is the name of the style that Dali moved to in the mid 20th century?

Salvador Dalí

Featured Artist

Salvador Dali was a Spanish **surrealist**, who lived from May 11th, 1904 to January 23rd, 1989. He was very well know for being a highly skilled **draftsman**. Dali is also well know for his technical skills, and his unique and other-worldly imagery. He was born in Figueres, Catalonia. He studied fine art in Mardid at the San Fernando Royal Academy of Fine Arts. From a very young age, he was influenced by the renaissance masters and the impressionists. He was also interested in **cubism** and the avante-garde movements in art. In the 1920's he developed more in the surrealist style and he went on to become a member of the surrealist group in 1929.

Rene Magritte, who had a great influence on Dali, and Dali's biggest rival, Pablo Picasso, were also artists contributing to the surrealist movement. Salvador Dali's most famous work was completed in 1940. It is called The Persistence of Memory. The painting features a deserted landscape with melting clocks, the distorted face of a man, ants, etc., The painting has been part of a permanent **exhibition** at the Museum of Modern Art (MOMA) in New York City, since 1934, after it was anonymously donated. Although Dali's most popular **medium** was oil painting, Dali has also created works in graphic art, photography and design, film, and sculpture.

During the Spanish Civil War, from 1936-1939, Dali lived in France. Afterwards, at the age of about 36 years old, Dali moved to the United States of America. He would receive great commercial success in America. In 1948, Dali returned to Catalonia and he began working on a new style which he called nuclear mysticism. Nuclear mysticism is a style that is inspired by quantum physics theories as well as theories of the subconscious mind.

Types of Movement

GLOSSARY	
color	Color can enhance the feeling of movement when high key (light in value and strong in chroma) and low key colors (dark and dull) are juxtaposed.
illusion	Some OP (optical) art creates movement with repetition and contrast.
implied	Artists create movement by changing the balance point and posture of a person. The artist can convey a static standing figure or the movement of a person walking or running.
lines	Movement is created using dynamic lines. Dynamic lines are often diagonal. They can also be zigzag or sweeping curves.

Caravaggio, Saint Matthew and the Angel 1602

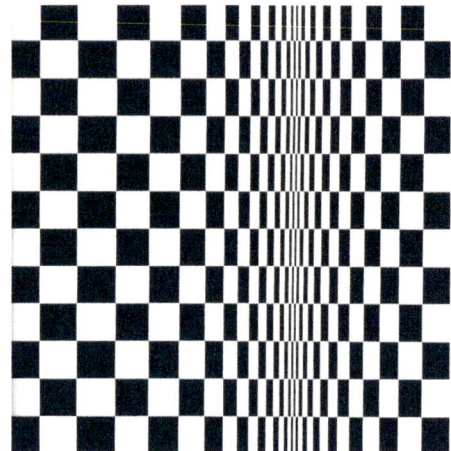

Bridge Riley, Movement in Squares 1961

Vasily Kandinsky, Blue Painting 1924

Juan Gris, Portrait of Pablo Picasso 1912

Victor Vasarely, Kdezi-Ga 1970©

Gabriele Münter, Portrait of Wassily Kandinsky 1906

Edgar Degas, The Dancer on Stage 1878

Paul Gris, Still Life with a Guitar 1911

Match the composition to the type of movement it has and explain why

1. Portrait of Pablo Picasso

2. Movement in Squares

3. Blue Painting

4. Saint Matthew and the Angel

5. Kdezi-Ga

6. Portrait of Wassily Kandinski

7. Still Life with a Guitar

8. The Dancer on Stage

Salvador Dali, Figure on the Rocks 1926

1. Comment on the type of movement that the painting has and then explain why it has that type of movement.

2. What is your opinion on this artwork, The Face of War by Salvador Dali? What do you think the meaning of it is?

Salvador Dali, Homage to Fox Newsreel 1926

1. Comment on the type of movement that the painting has and then explain why it has that type of movement.

2. What is your opinion on this artwork, Temptation of Saint Anthony by Salvador Dali? What do you think the meaning of it is?

Salvador Dali, Three Figures 1926

1. What is in the **foreground** of the painting?

2. What is in the **background** of the painting?

3. What is the **focal point** of the painting?

4. What **focal point method** was used?

5. What is the **scene** in the painting of?

6. What type of **balance** does the painting have? Why?

7. Why is there **tension** in the painting? How is it created?

8. What type of **rhythm** does the painting have? Why?

9. What is your opinion of this **style** of painting?

10. How is **harmony** represented with shapes?

11. Are the colors mainly **high key**, **mid key** or **low key**? Why?

12. Comment on the **emphasis** that the painting has.

13. Comment on the **proportion**.

14. Comment on the type of **movement** that the painting has and why.

SURREALISM THE BIG IDEAS

ANSWER THE GAP FILL QUESTIONS

1. People use the word _____ to describe things that are crazy.

2. But surrealism was about more than just melting clocks. It was about _____, _____, _____, and revolution.

3. A group of people who focused on the world of _____. In order to create a new _____. A reality that was beyond real, or _____.

4. Soldiers watched whole _____ crumble.

5. By the end of the war, almost _____ million people were injured, imprisoned, missing, or dead.

6. The war made people question their own _____.

7. They did everything they could to disrupt _____.

8. But after months of experimental _____.

9. When he woke up, he realized that we're not in control of everything that goes on in our _____.

10. There is a _____ part. A disorderly _____ , and this is called the _____.

11. The conscious mind contains the _____ that we are aware of.

12. The unconscious mind communicates through _____ in our dreams.

13. After writers, _____ joined the group.

14. Elements like, _____, juxtaposition, and _____.

15. Turning the uncomfortable parts of his life into _____ visions that audiences couldn't look away from.

GOING INTO THE SUBCONSCIOUS MIND

Salvador Dali, Honey is Sweeter than Blood 1926

Write about the plan for a surrealistic painting

1. What or who is the subject?

2. What are the subjects doing, what is the type of *movement used?*

3. What is the deeper meaning of the actions?

4. What is the color palate of the painting? Why?

5. What makes the design surrealistic?

Winsor McCay, Little Nemo , 1907

VARIETY

Creating visual interest by slightly changing or using different elements together in a composition. It can be created with contrast, and elaboration of different elements.

VARIETY 7

MUSINGS

1. Pop culture and pop music both have the word "pop", why is that?

2. "Variety is the spice of life" is an American saying, what do you think it means?

3. Do you think that variety is important in art? Yes or no and why or why not?

GLOSSARY

advertise-ment	the graphic design used to advertise and promote such as photography, illustrations, etc.,
art move-ment	style in art with a specific common philosophy or goal, followed by a group of artists during a specific period of time
comic strip	a sequence of drawings in boxes that tell an amusing story, typically printed in a newspaper or comic book
commercial printing	a process of taking artwork and transferring it onto a piece of paper or card. It can be used to produce a wide variety of products: brochures, books, flyers, invitations, magazines, newsletters, catalogues, and more
pop art	art based on modern popular culture and the mass media, especially as a critical or ironic comment on traditional fine art values.

FILL IN THE BLANK WITH THE CORRECT VOCABULARY WORD

1. Andy Warhol is very well known for making _____ of Marilyn Monroe.

2. Companies often put product _____ onto movie sets.

3. The _____ was very popular with the young, Korean boys because of the many action scenes.

4. The class studied different _____ for their research projects.

5. She loved her job at the new _____ business because the machines were more modern.

READING COMPREHENSION

1. What is Winsor McCay best known for?

2. In what way was McCay's work different from other comic strips of his time?

3. What other areas of art and design did McCay work in, aside from comic strips and animation?

4. How is Winsor McCay's work viewed today in the art world?

5. Are McCay's works currently protected by copyright?

Winsor McCay

Winsor McCay was an American cartoonist and animator who is widely regarded as one of the most innovative and influential artists in the history of **comic strips**. McCay began his career in the late 19th century working in **commercial printing**, but soon found his true passion in the field of illustration and art. In the early 20th century, McCay became one of the pioneers of the **art movement** known as the "Golden Age of American Animation". He created a number of groundbreaking animated shorts, including the wildly popular "Gertie the Dinosaur", which was a sensation in its time.

McCay is perhaps best known for his comic strip "Little Nemo in Slumberland", which he began in 1905. The strip was characterized by its richly detailed and imaginative dreamscapes, which were a stark departure from the more mundane and formulaic comic strips of the era. McCay's attention to detail and his unique use of color and composition helped to establish him as a true master of the art form. In addition to his work in animation and comic strips, McCay was also involved in commercial printing and **advertisement**, creating eye-catching illustrations and advertisements for a number of different companies. Today, McCay's work continues to be celebrated for its technical and artistic innovation, and is considered a precursor to the **pop art** movement of the mid-20th century.

Adding Variety to work

GLOSSARY	
elaboration	extra information; more details
contrast	the arrangement of opposite elements (light versus dark, rough versus smooth textures, large versus small shapes, color, scale, etc., to create visual interest.

CONTRAST

COLOR   SHAPE   SCALE

Gustav Klimt, detail The Kiss 1907-1908

Janis Rozentāls, After Church 1894

Michael Pacher, Saint Wolfgang and the Devil 1475

Okamoto Shuki, untitled 19th

1. Identify the type(s) of variety used in the Gustave Klimt painting and explain why.

2. Identify the type(s) of variety used in the Janis Rozentāls painting and explain why.

3. Identify the type(s) of variety used in the Michael Pacher painting and explain why.

4. Identify the type(s) of variety used in the Okamoto Shuki painting and explain why.

Winsor McCay, Little Nemo 1905

1. Specifically, how could this composition be elaborated to create more variety?

2. Specifically, in what way could additional contrast create more variety?

3. In your opinion, what sort of addition to this artwork would detract (take away) from its aesthetics?

4. What is your opinion of the current piece? Do you like it or dislike it? Why? What do you like or dislike about it?

DIALOGUE BUILDING

To create more variety in the composition, the artwork could be elaborated by...

To create more variety in the composition, the artwork could have more contrast added by...

In my opinion, the artwork would be ruined if there was/were_____ added... because...

I think that the artwork is...
I like/dislike the composition because.. .

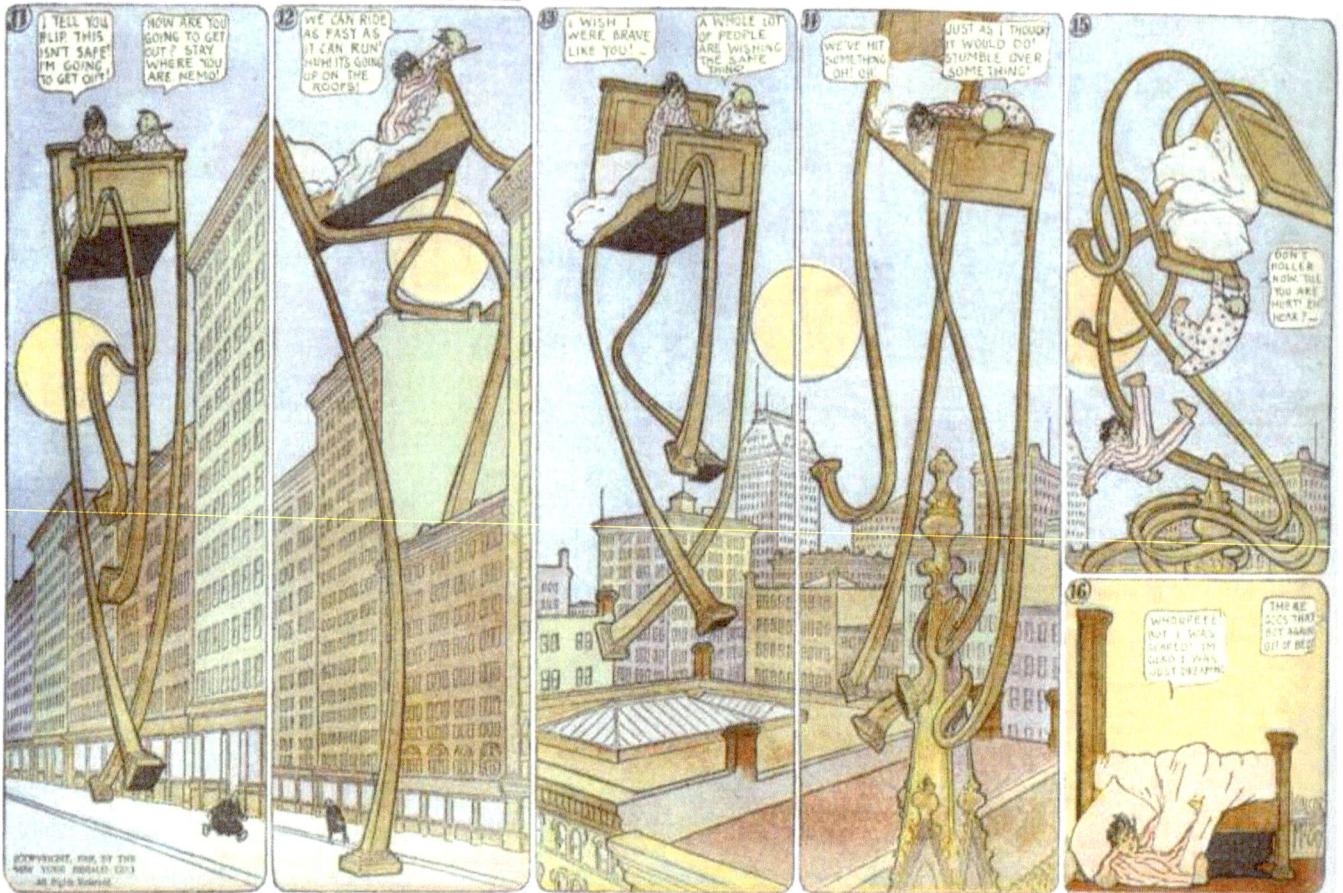

Winsor McCay, Little Nemo 1908

1. Specifically, how could this composition be elaborated to create more variety?

2. Specifically, in what way could additional contrast create more variety?

3. In your opinion, what sort of addition to this artwork would detract (take away) from its aesthetics?

4. What is your opinion of the current piece? Do you like it or dislike it? Why? What do you like or dislike about it?

DIALOGUE BUILDING

To create more variety in the composition, the artwork could be elaborated by...

To create more variety in the composition, the artwork could have more contrast added by...

In my opinion, the artwork would be ruined if there was/were_____ added... because...

I think that the artwork is...
I like/dislike the composition because.. .

Winsor McCay, Little Nemo 1907

1. What is in the **foreground** of the painting?

2. What is in the **background** of the painting?

3. What is the **focal point** of the painting?

4. What **focal point method** was used?

5. What is the **scene** in the painting of?

6. What type of **balance** does the painting have? Why?

7. Why is there **tension** in the painting? How is it created?

8. What type of **rhythm** does the painting have? Why?

9. What is your opinion of this **style** of painting?

10. How is **harmony** represented with shapes?

11. Are the colors mainly **high key**, **mid key** or **low key**? Why?

12. Comment on the **emphasis** that the painting has.

13. Comment on the **proportion**.

14. Comment on the type of **movement** that the painting has and why.

15. How is **variety** used in the painting?

Winsor McCay, untitled 20th

THE CHILDREN OF IGNORANCE

Winsor McCay, untitled 20th

THE ART AND IMAGINATION OF WINSOR MCCAY

A Precursor to Pop Art

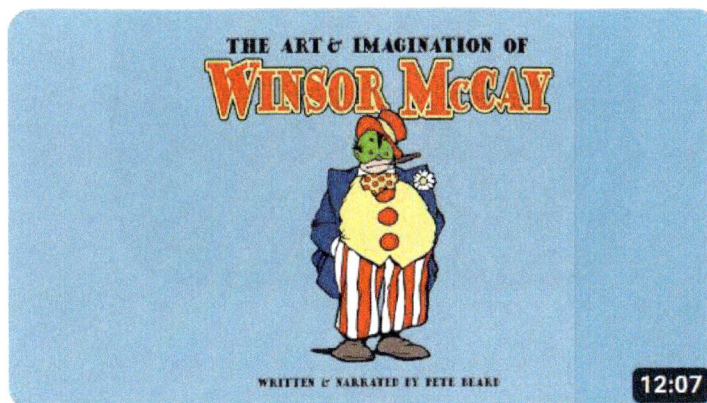

POP ART: THE EXCHANGE OF CREATIVITY AND CULTURE

ANSWER THE MULTIPLE CHOICE QUESTIONS

1. Pop art was a reaction to the

    A. impressionism movement   **B.** art movement

    C. expressionism movement   **D.** abstract expressionism movement

2. Pop art was born in England and

    A. New York   **B.** California

    C. Chicago   **D.** Texas

3. Pop arts origins can be traced back to

    A. 1918   **B.** 2012

    C. 1930   **D.** 1917

4. Pop art in the 50s and 60s can be seen in some of the

    A. music   **B.** fashion

    C. interior design   **D.** history books

5. Pop art paintings involved the use of existing imagery from mass culture borrowed from

    A. photography   **B.** French culture

    C. comic strips   **D.** advertising

6. Pop art merged the realm of high art and

    A. American culture   **B.** culture

    C. English culture   **D.** popular culture

Pablo Picasso, The Old Guitarist 1903-1904

LINE

Lines and curves are marks that span a distance between two points (or the path of a moving point). As an element of visual art, line is the use of various marks, outlines, and implied lines during artwork and design. A line has a width, direction, curve, and length. A line's width is most times called its "thickness". Lines are sometimes called "strokes", especially when referring to lines in digital artwork.

LINE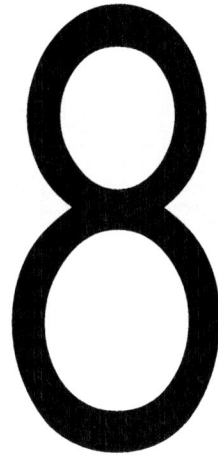

MUSINGS

1. When children first learn to draw, they usually scribble, why do you think that is?

2. What is the meaning of doodle? Do you ever doodle? If so, when?

3. Do you enjoy anime or comic book art? If so, who are your favorite characters?

GLOSSARY

abstraction   A form of art that emphasizes non-representational or non-realistic elements.

Avant garde   A term used to describe new or experimental art, often associated with being ahead of its time.

color theory   The study of how colors interact with each other and how they can be used in art and design.

sculpture   A three-dimensional form of art created by carving, molding, or casting.

symbolism   The use of symbols to represent ideas or qualities.

FILL IN THE BLANK WITH THE CORRECT VOCABULARY WORD

1. The _____ refers to those ahead of their time.

2. _____ helps with color selection and design.

3. _____ involves shaping raw materials into something new.

4. _____ uses symbols to represent ideas or concepts.

5. The tree was drawn not based on the way that it looks in reality, it was drawn as an _____

READING COMPREHENSION

1. In which city did Picasso become part of the avant-garde art scene?

2. What art movement is Picasso known for being a founder of?

3. What is Cubism?

4. What is Picasso's legacy in the art world?

5. When did Picasso die?

Pablo Picasso

Pablo Picasso was a Spanish artist who lived in the 19th and 20th centuries and is widely regarded as one of the most influential artists of the modern era. He was born in Malaga, Spain, in 1881 and showed an early talent for art. He moved to Paris in his early twenties, where he became a part of the thriving **avant-garde** art scene. Picasso is known for his diverse range of styles and techniques, as well as his innovative approach to art. He is widely recognized as one of the founders of the Cubist movement, which emphasized the fragmentation and **abstraction** of forms. Picasso's works often contained complex **symbolism**, and he was known for his use of **color theory** and his explorations of different mediums, including **sculpture** and printmaking.

Throughout his career, Picasso produced thousands of works of art, including paintings, sculptures, ceramics, and prints. His legacy has continued to inspire and influence artists around the world, and his works are still widely celebrated and studied today. Picasso died in 1973 at the age of 91, leaving behind a profound impact on the art world.

contour lines	lines that show the outlines, shapes, and edges of a scene, but often omits fine detail, surface texture, color, and tone.
cross contour lines	contains parallel lines that run across the surface of an object (or radiate from a central point), such as those that appear on a topographical map or a digital wireframe.
cross hatching	intersecting sets of parallel lines
curved lines	a line that is not straight
diagonal lines	lines that slant
hatching	long, parallel lines on an angle
horizontal	lines that are parallel to the horizon
length	lines can be long or short
parallel	two lines on a plane that never meet
scribbles	lines that are drawn carelessly and quickly
spiral	winding in a continuous and gradually widening (or tightening) curve, around a central point on a flat plane.
stippling	numerous small dots or specks
texture	lines can be rough or smooth
vertical	lines that move up and down without any slant
width	lines can be wide or narrow
zigzag	lines made from a combination of diagonal lines

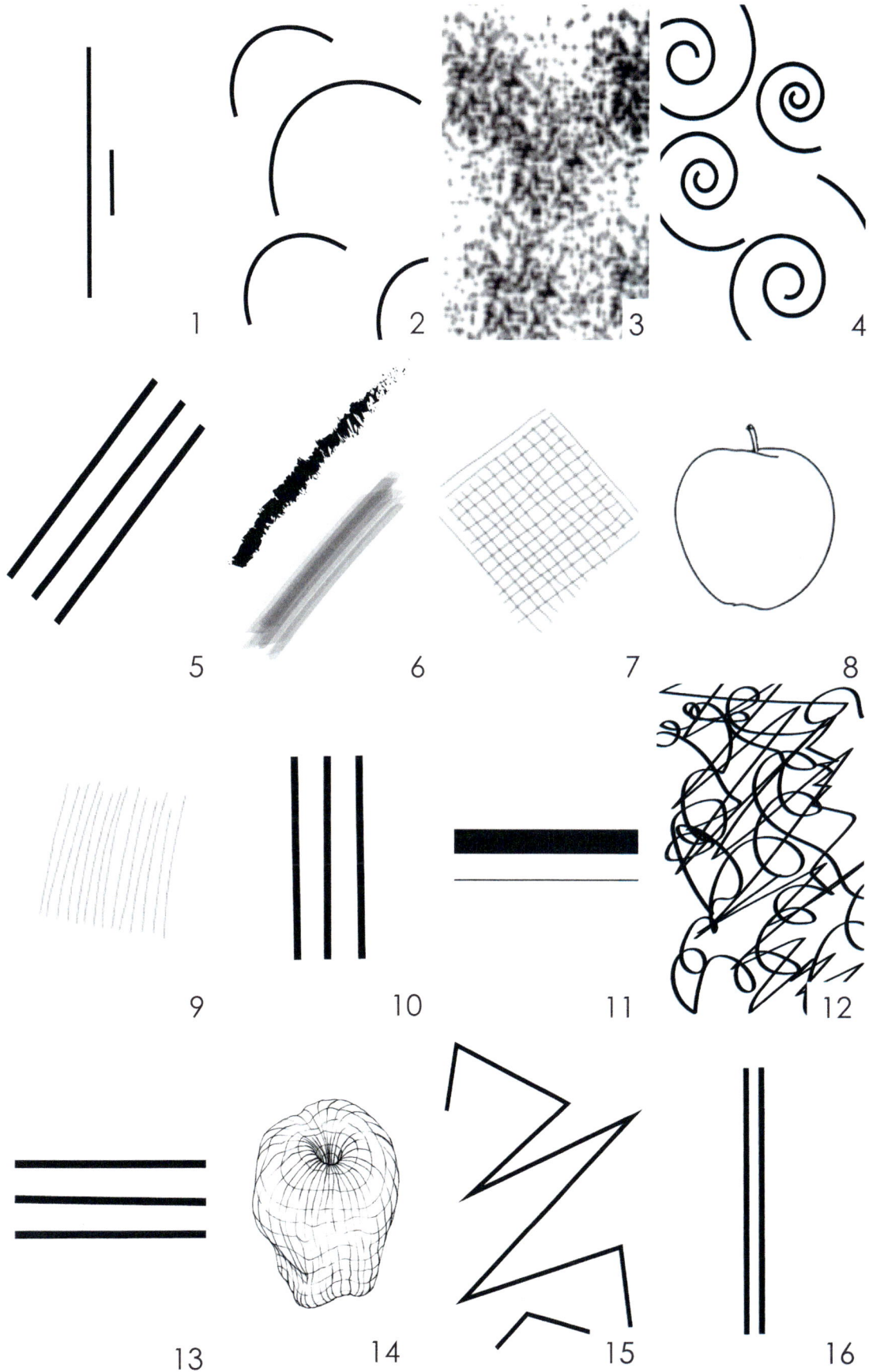

TYPES OF LINE

1

2

3

4

5

6

7

8

9

10

11

12

13

14

15

16

Describe the type of line techniques used in each picture

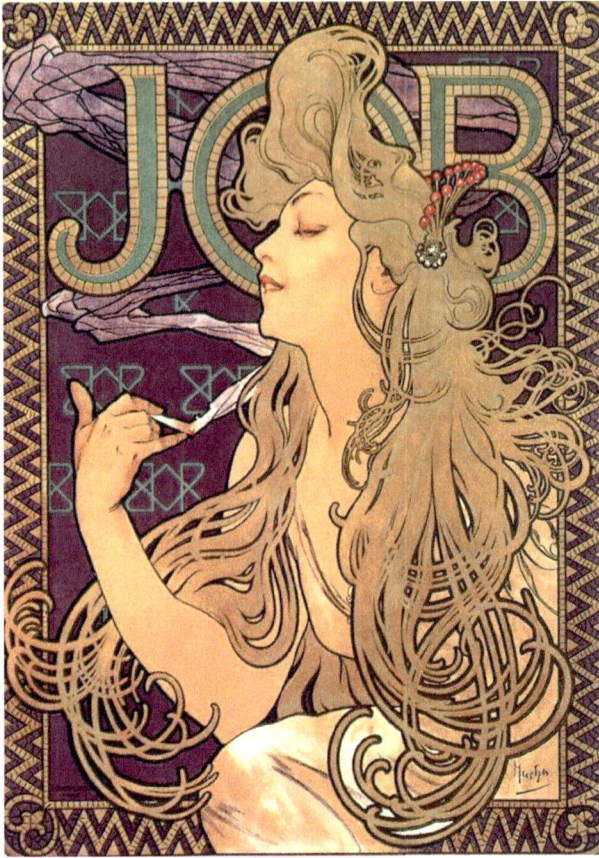

Alphonse Mucha, Poster for Job Cigarettes 1898

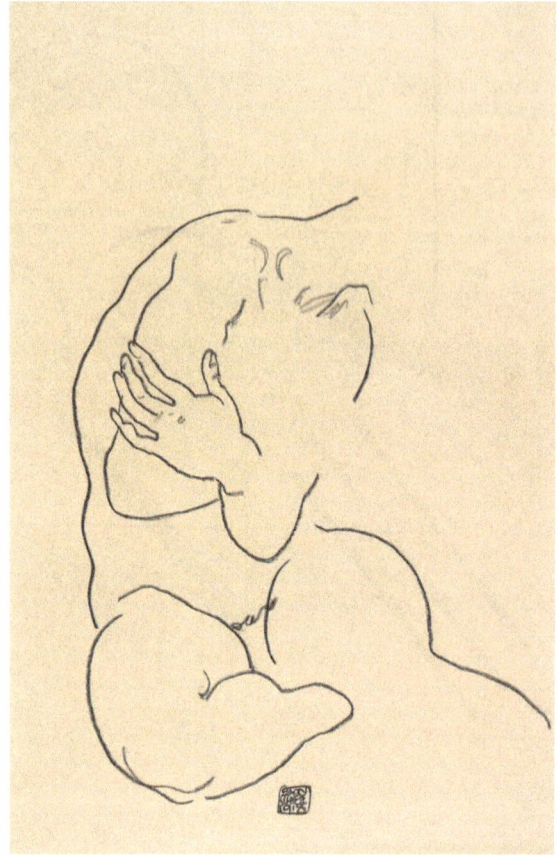

Egon Schiele, sitting female torso 1918

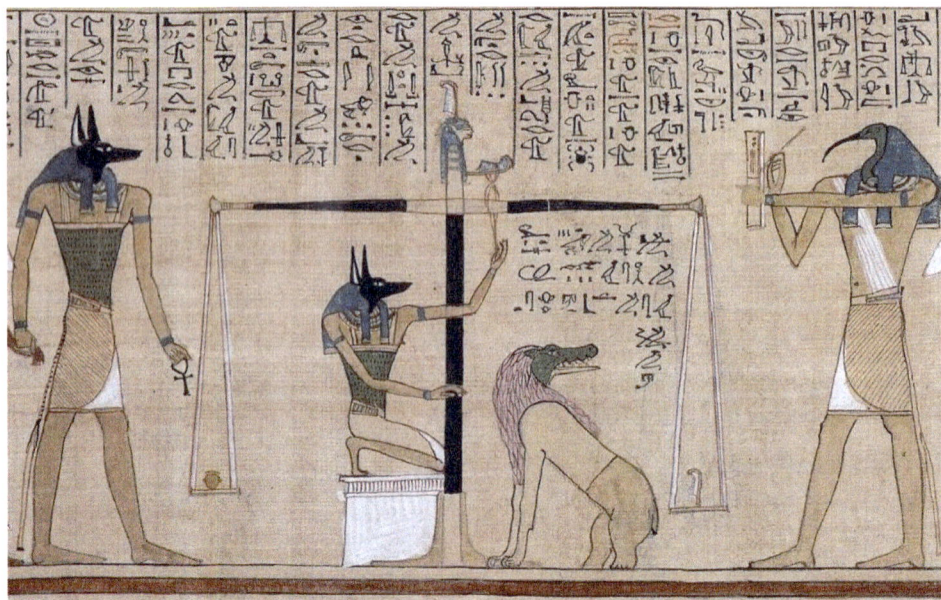

Egyptian Book of the Dead, 1275 BCE

Vincent Van Gogh, Wheatfield and Cypresses 1889

Courtney Cornelius Adams, Art Class 3030 ©

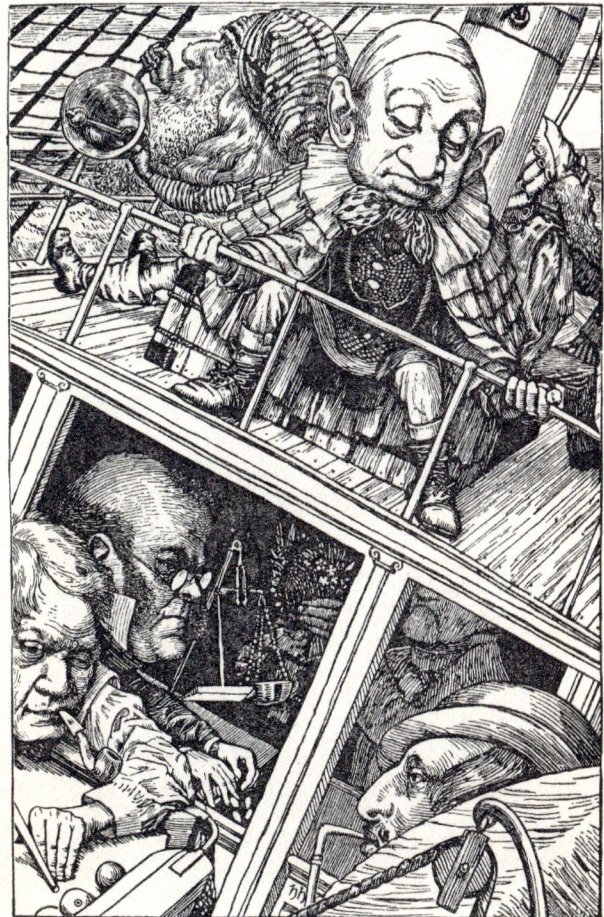

Henry Holiday, The Hunting of the Snark 1876

Pablo Picasso, Three Musicians 1921

1. Discuss the line techniques used in the Three Musicians 1921 piece.

2. Discuss the line techniques used in the Bottle of Vieux Marc, Glass, Guitar, and Newspaper 1913 piece.

4. What do find *interesting* or *unusual* about the way that the artist, Picasso, used line techniques to create the images?

Pablo Picasso, Bottle of Vieux Marc, Glass, Guitar, and Newspaper 1913

Pablo Picasso, The Women of Avignon 1907

1. What is in the **foreground** of the painting?

2. What is in the **background** of the painting?

3. What is the **focal point** of the painting?

4. What **focal point method** was used?

5. What is the **scene** in the painting of?

6. What type of **balance** does the painting have? Why?

7. Why is there **tension** in the painting? How is it created?

8. What type of **rhythm** does the painting have? Why?

9. What is your opinion of this **style** of painting?

10. How is **harmony** represented with shapes?

11. Are the colors mainly **high key**, **mid key** or **low key**? Why?

12. Comment on the **emphasis** that the painting has.

13. Comment on the **proportion**.

14. Comment on the type of **movement** that the painting has and why.

15. How is **variety** used in the painting?

16. Comment on the types of **line** techniques used.

ART NOUVEAU – OVERVIEW – GOODBYE ART ACADEMY

ANSWER THE LISTENING COMPREHENSION QUESTIONS

1. When did art take an academic turn?

2. What did people have to do to be considered a serious artist?

3. What is the name of the very short, but highly influential art movement?

4. What does art nouveau mean?

5. Art nouveau moved away from the imitation of real subjects and moved towards what?

6. What do art historians call the designs that "decorate every surface"?

7. What became the new inspiration for European artists?

8. What are both prominent features of Japanese prints and art nouveau designs?

9. What were used as artist's reference books?

10. What was "passionately challenged" during this movement?

11. Art nouveau was the first artistic movement to give serious credibility to what?

12. What is one of Alphonse Mucha's best known works?

13. What is the name of the artist with the "immensely popular" posters?

14. How long did art nouveau last?

15. What movements followed art nouveau?

Conveying Emotion with Line

A

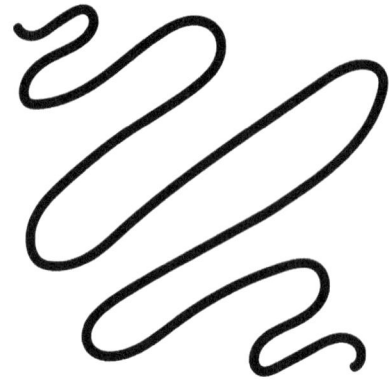

B

C

D

E

F

jealousy   anger   calm

excited   anxiety   joy

DISCUSSION

1. How can line techniques convey emotion?

2. What does each emotion mean? When do people have these emotions?

3. Each of the line drawings is associated with one of the emotions. Which emotion does you associate with each line drawing and why?

4. Which of the artists from this unit do you think has the most expressive lines? Why?

Vincent Van Gogh, Café Terrace at Night 1888

COLOR

Color is the element of art that is produced when light, striking an object, is reflected to the eye. There are three properties to color. The first is hue, which simply means the name we give to a color (red, yellow, blue, green, etc.). The second property is intensity, which refers to the vividness of the color. A color's intensity is sometimes referred to as its "colorfulness", its "saturation", its "purity" or its "strength". The third and final property of color is its value, meaning how light or dark it is. The terms shade and tint refer to value changes in colors. In painting, shades are created by adding black to a color, while tints are created by adding white to a color.

COLOR 9

"I am seeking, I am striving, I am in it with all my heart."
-Vincent Van Gogh

MUSINGS

1. Do you believe that the psychological state of a person can be influenced by the color of their environment? Yes or no and why or why not?

2. What is your favorite color? Why? What is your least favorite color? Why?

3. Why do you think that colors are important when an artist is creating a composition?

GLOSSARY

billboard	a large outdoor board for displaying advertisements
conceptual artist	an artist who creates art which emphasizes the process and the meaning of the art rather than the finished product
collaborated	to work jointly on an activity, especially to produce or create something
studio	a room where an artist, photographer, sculptor, etc. works
visionary artist	artist that transcends the physical world and portrays a wider vision of awareness including spiritual or mystical themes, or is based in such experiences

FILL IN THE BLANK WITH THE CORRECT VOCABULARY WORD

1. The famous artists _____ on the painting together and profited well.

2. The _____ studied philosophy and he was a very creative thinker.

3. The people in the neighborhood hated the new _____ because it was an eyesore.

4. The painter dreamed of having a _____ to call his own for ten years.

5. The _____ of the Buddhists showed the realm of the living and the dead.

READING COMPREHENSION

1. Who was Vincent van Gogh?

2. What was his artistic style?

3. What did Van Gogh believe about the role of art in the world?

4. Where did Van Gogh work and what did he produce there?

5. What is Van Gogh's legacy and how is his work recognized today?

Vincent van Gogh

Featured Artist

Vincent van Gogh was a Dutch artist who lived from 1853 to 1890. He is considered one of the most significant and influential artists of the 19th century, and his work had a profound impact on the development of modern art. Van Gogh was a **conceptual artist** who explored the use of color, light, and form to create a unique visual language. His work was deeply influenced by his personal experiences and emotions, and he sought to capture the essence of the world around him through his art. Van Gogh was also a **visionary artist** who believed that art could transcend its traditional boundaries and become a means of expressing the deepest truths about the human experience. He saw his art as a means of connecting with the spiritual and emotional aspects of life and sought to create works that would move and inspire others.

Van Gogh worked primarily in his **studio**, where he produced a vast number of paintings, drawings, and sketches throughout his career. He **collaborated** with other artists, including Paul Gauguin, during his time in Arles, where they worked together and exchanged ideas. Despite his immense talent, Van Gogh struggled to gain recognition during his lifetime and lived in poverty for much of his career. However, his legacy has endured, and his work is celebrated today for its beauty, originality, and emotional power. In recent years, Van Gogh's work has even been featured on **billboards** and other public spaces, reaching a wider audience than ever before and proving that his art continues to resonate with people around the world.

GLOSSARY

color (hue)	light in different wavelengths striking the eyes
intensity	the brightness of a color; a color is at full intensity when not mixed with black or white - a pure hue
value	the degree of lightness and darkness in a color

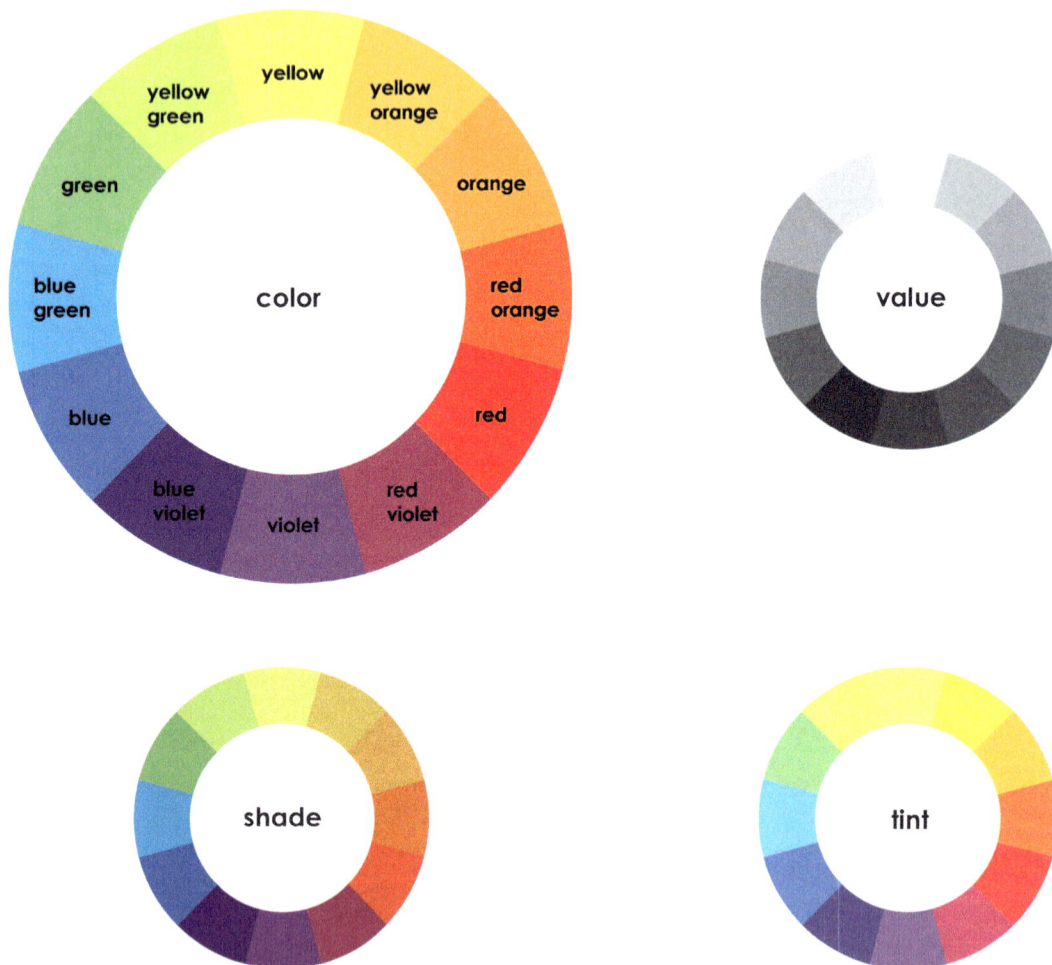

GLOSSARY

shade	adding black to a color
tint	adding white to a color

GLOSSARY	
primary color	any of a group of colors from which all other colors can be obtained by mixing
secondary color	a color resulting from the mixing of two primary colors
tertiary color	an equal mixture of a primary color with a secondary color next to it on the color wheel

GROUP 1

GROUP 2

GROUP 3

DISCUSSION

1. What colors does group 1 represent?

2. What colors does group 2 represent?

3. Which primary colors create orange?

4. Which primary colors create purple?

5. Which primary colors create green?

6. How many tertiary colors are there on the color wheel?

GLOSSARY	
analogous	any one of a group of related colors that are near each other on the color wheel
complementary	colors located across from each other on the color wheel (one primary color, and the color opposite on the wheel, the secondary color); when placed next to each other, they create the strongest contrast for those two colors
split complimentary	three colors that are side by side on the color wheel and the color that lies directly across the color wheel from the color at the center of the trio
tetradic	all four colors are distributed around the color wheel, creating no clear dominance of one color
triadic	three colors evenly spaced on the color wheel

DISCUSSION

1. Which type of color does number 1 represent? Why?

2. Which type of color does number 2 represent? Why?

3. Which type of color does number 3 represent? Why?

4. Which type of color does number 4 represent? Why?

5. Which type of color does number 5 represent? Why?

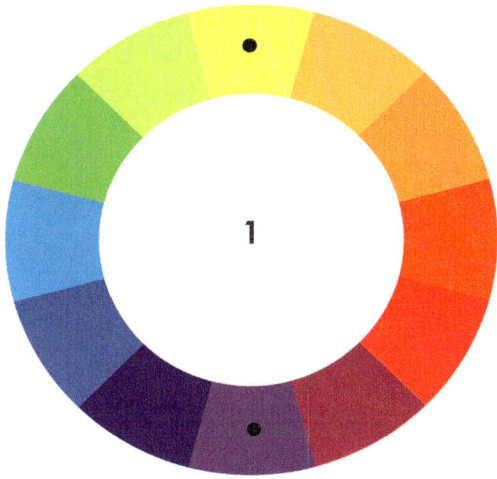

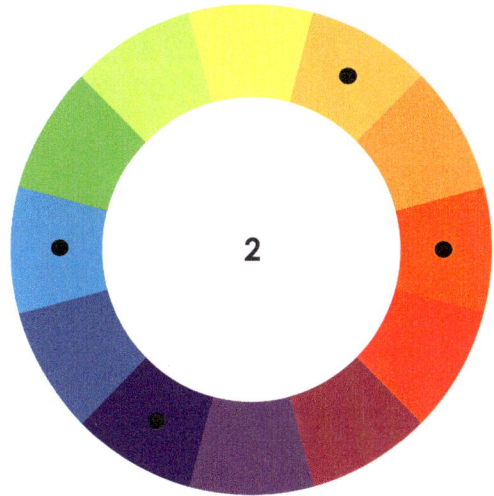

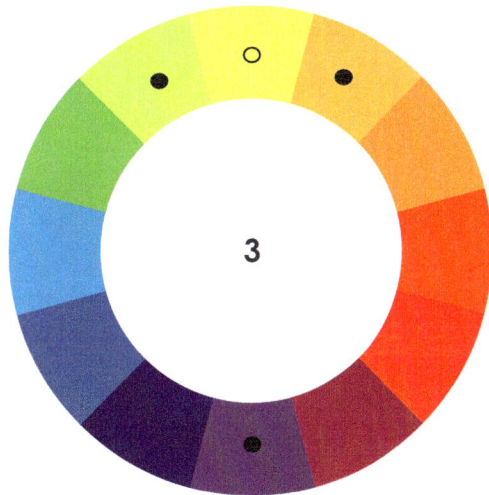

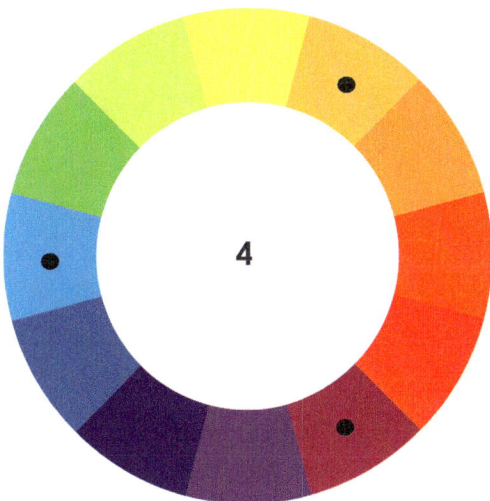

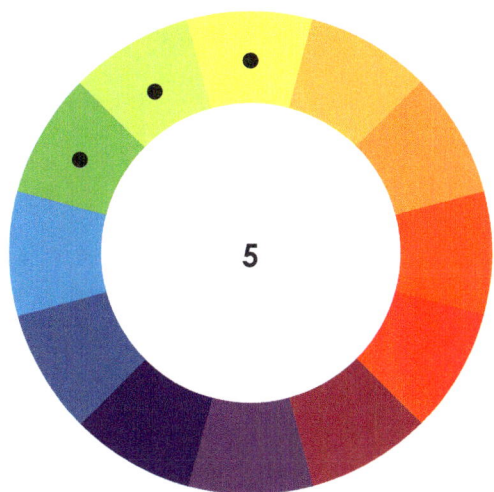

GLOSSARY

cool colors   cool colors are made with blue, green, purple, or some combination of these

neutral colors don't usually show up on the color wheel. Neutral colors include black, white, gray, and sometimes brown and beige. They are sometimes called "earth tones."

warm colors   warm colors are made with red, orange, yellow, or some combination of these

Louis Anquetin Inside Bruant's Mirliton 1867-1868

Georges Seurat The Circus 1891

Vincent Van Gogh Wheatfield Under Thunderclouds 1890

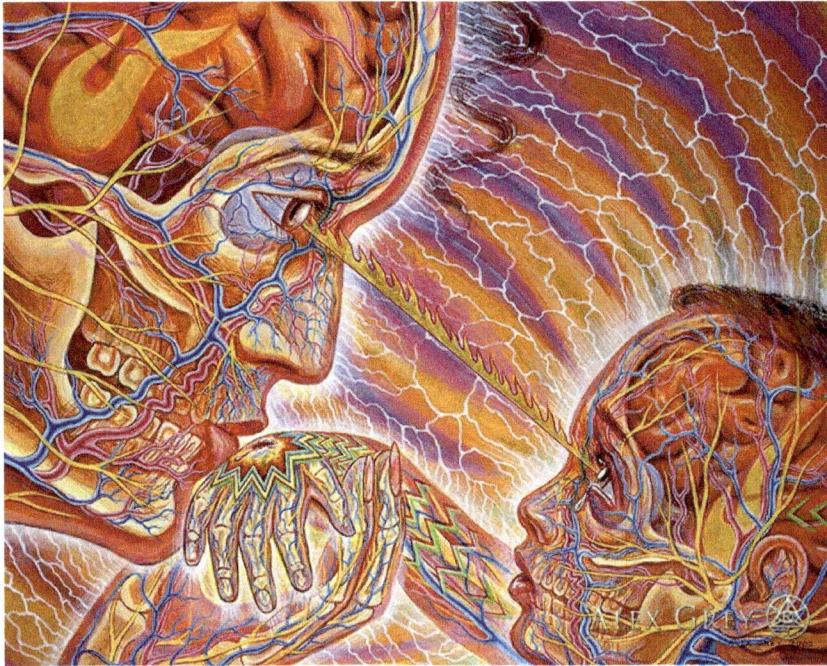

Alex Grey, Boo Boo 2002

Vincent Van Gogh Sunflowers 1888

William Bruce Ranken Adam's Work 20th

1. Which painting shows analogous colors? Why?

2. Which painting shows cool colors? Why?

3. Which painting shows warm colors? Why?

4. Which painting shows neutral colors? Why?

5. Which painting shows complimentary colors? Why?

6. Which painting shows tints and shades of blue and green? Why?

Vincent Van Gogh, The Potato Eaters 1885

1. Discuss the color techniques used in the Tantra painting.

2. Discuss the color techniques used in the Kissing painting.

Vincent Van Gogh, Irises 1889

Vincent Van Gogh, The Bedroom 1889

1. What is in the **foreground** of the painting?

2. What is in the **background** of the painting?

3. What is the **focal point** of the painting?

4. What **focal point method** was used?

5. What is the **scene** in the painting of?

6. What type of **balance** does the painting have? Why?

7. Why is there **tension** in the painting? How is it created?

8. What type of **rhythm** does the painting have? Why?

9. What is your opinion of this **style** of painting?

10. How is **harmony** represented with shapes?

11. Are the colors mainly **high key**, **mid key** or **low key**? Why?

12. Comment on the **emphasis** that the painting has.

13. Comment on the **proportion**.

14. Comment on the type of **movement** that the painting has and why.

15. How is **variety** used in the painting?

16. Comment on the types of **line** techniques used.

17. Comment on the **color** technique used in the painting.

COLOR THEORY VINCENT VAN GOGH

ANSWER THE MULTIPLE CHOICE QUESTIONS

1. Color theory is the study of _____.

    A. objects   **C.** contrast

    B. color   **D.** science

2. Van Gogh was a difficult artist to work with because he suffered from _____.

    A. many illnesses   **C.** lazy habits

    B. overcoming shyness   **D.** madness

3. Van Gogh cut off his own _____.

    A. foot   **C.** finger

    B. ear   **D.** toe

4. Van Gogh is now regarded as one of the greatest _____ ever.

    A. thinkers   **C.** painters

    B. drawers   **D.** expressionists

5. I use color more _____ in order to express myself more _____.

    A. forcefully/immediately   **C.** arbitrarily/expressively

    B. arbitrarily/forcefully   **D.** quickly/readily

6. In Van Gogh's Irises, he created tension and contrast through the use of _____.

    A. split colors   **C.** hues

    B. contrasting colors   **D.** complementary colors

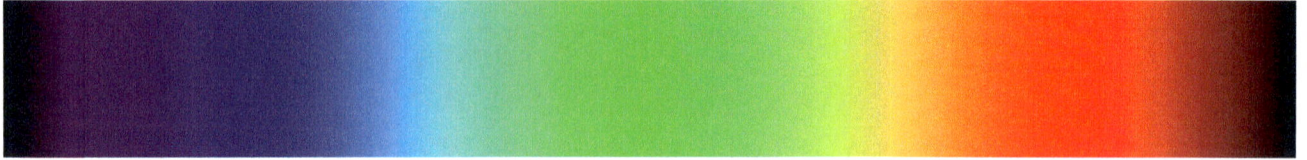

SPECTRUM OF VISIBLE LIGHT

Color	Wavelength	Frequency	Photon energy
Violet	380–450 nm	670–790 THz	2.75–3.26 eV
Blue	450–485 nm	620–670 THz	2.56–2.75 eV
Cyan	485–500 nm	600–620 THz	2.48–2.56 eV
Green	500–565 nm	530–600 THz	2.19–2.48 eV
Yellow	565–590 nm	510–530 THz	2.10–2.19 eV
Orange	590–625 nm	480–510 THz	1.98–2.10 eV
Red	625–700 nm	400–480 THz	1.65–1.98 eV

Color has the ability to influence the psychological state of people. Take the quizzes and see what you can learn about color and yourself that you didn't know before.

- After taking the quizzes, answer the discussion questions below

Color Code Personality Test

DIRECTIONS:

PART 1 Strengths and Limitations

Section 1 has 30, 4 word clusters. For each cluster, pick the one word that best describes how you were *as a child*.

PART 2 Situations

Section 2 has 15 different situations with four possible reactions for each section. As in section 1, respond according to how you would have responded *as a child*.

Color Quiz

DIRECTIONS:

Part 1 Pick the colors that make you feel best

Pick the 8 colors from your most favorite color to your least favorite color

Part 2 Pick the colors again after the countdown

Pick the 8 colors again from your most favorite color to your least favorite color

DISCUSSION

1, What parts of the *color code* analysis seems accurate?

2, What parts of the *color code* analysis seem very inaccurate and don't reflect who you are as a person?

3. What parts of the analysis from the *color quiz* do you think are accurate?

4. Which parts of the *color quiz* analysis seem very inaccurate and don't reflect who you are as a person?

Leonardo Da Vinci, sketch 15th-16th

FORM

The form of a work is its shape, including its volume or perceived volume. A three-dimensional artwork has depth as well as width and height. Three-dimensional form is the basis of sculpture. However, two-dimensional artwork can achieve the illusion of form with the use of perspective and/or shading or modeling techniques.

FORM # 10

MUSINGS

1. What is the difference between a two dimensional shape and a three dimensional shape?

2. What do you already know about light and shadow?

3. Why do you think that after over 500 years, half a millennium, Leonardo Da Vinci is still one of the most well known artists?

GLOSSARY

apprentice	a person who learns a job or skill by working for a fixed period of time for someone who is very good at that job or skill
commis-sioned	to order or request (something) to be made or done for payment
patron	a person who gives money and support to an artist, organization, etc.,
Renaissance man	a man who is interested in and knows a lot about many things
smufato	in painting or drawing, the fine shading that produces soft, imperceptible transitions between colors and tones

FILL IN THE BLANK WITH THE CORRECT VOCABULARY WORD

1. For the lesson on _____, the instructor used close up details of the artwork to try and find the brush strokes.

2. The wealthy lady invested a lot of money as a _____ of the arts.

3. The interior designer _____ a huge painting for the area behind the sofa.

4. The _____ was told to do more listening than speaking when on the job.

5. It seemed like he knew everything! He was a true _____.

READING COMPREHENSION

1. Where was Leonardo Da Vinci born?

2. What is known about Da Vinci's mother?

3. Who was Da Vinci the apprentice of?

4. Why was being a master in the Guild of Saint Luke necessary as an artist?

5. What are the infamous paintings called?

Leonardo Da Vinci

Featured Artist

Leonardo Da Vinci was born on the 14th or the 15th of April in 1452 and he died on the 2nd of May in 1519. His nationality is Italian. He was born in the Tuscan town of Vinci. The art movement that Da Vinci belongs to is called the High Renaissance period. The High Renaissance period is known for its advancement in painting style. Some of the advancements included linear perspective, painting realistic physical features, **smufato**, and chiaroscuro (contrast between light and dark). The early life of Da Vinci was challenging as he was born the illegitimate child of a wealthy notary named Messer Piero Fruosino di Antonio Da Vinci and a peasant named Caterina. Not much is known about Da Vinci's mother except that she was impoverished and possibly a local youth. Da Vinci received an informal education in Latin, geometry, and mathematics. At approximately the age of 14 he became a studio boy (garzone).

He worked in the workshop of the famous painter Andrea del Verrocchio, who was a very popular Florentine painter at the time. About 3 years later, Leonardo Da Vinci became the **apprentice** of Verrocchio. He trained with Verrocchio for 7 years. At the young age of 20, Leonardo Da Vinci qualified for a positon of distinction. The positon was as a master in the Guild of Saint Luke, the guild of artists and doctors of medicine. A guild is a medieval association of craftsmen or merchants, often having considerable power. This meant that, in order for an artist to take on apprentices or sell artwork to the public, they had to be a master of the Guild of Saint Luke. During the Renaissance period, religion was extremely important because the church was the authoritative source of information about heaven and earth. Because of this, a lot of the content of the work that was **commissioned** from Leonardo Da Vinci has a religious theme, such as the Madonna and Child. Da Vinci had art **patrons** that ranged from monks, to the very rich noblemen and women in Italy at the time. One such painting, perhaps the most famous painting in the world, is the infamous Mona Lisa. The painting is likely of the Italian noblewoman Lisa Gherardini, the wife of Francesco del Giocondo. Another infamous painting of Leonardo Da Vinci's is The Last Supper, which is one of the western world's most recognized paintings. Leonardo achieved much recognition and success as an artist during his lifetime. Da Vinci will forever be known as the **Renaissance man** who was also an inventor, who was interested in mathematics, science, architecture, anatomy, music, engineering, literature, geology, astronomy, botany, paleontology, and cartography.

GLOSSARY

circle	a perfectly round shape
cone	a shape that has a pointed top and sides that form a circle at the bottom.
cube	a shape that has six square sides
cylinder	a shape that has straight sides and two circular ends
hexagonal pyramid	a pyramid with hexagonal base and six triangular faces
pyramid	a shape that is wide near the bottom and narrows gradually as it reaches the top
rectangle	a four sided shape that is made up of two pairs of parallel lines and that has four right angles
sphere	a three-dimensional shape that looks like a ball
square	a four-sided shape that is made up of four straight sides that are the same length and that has four right angles
triangle	a shape that is made up of three lines and three angles

Match the form to the vocabulary term

1. cylinder

2. sphere

3. pyramid

4. cone

5. cube

6. hexagonal pyramid

BASIC GEOMETRIC 2-D and 3-D FORMS

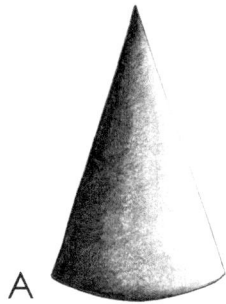

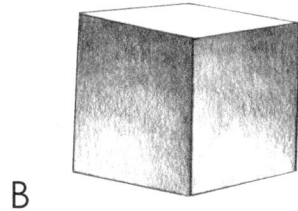

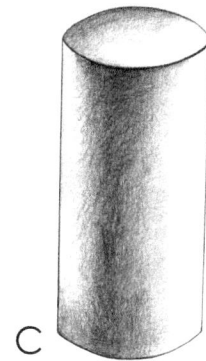

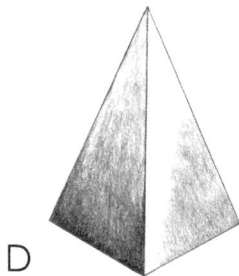

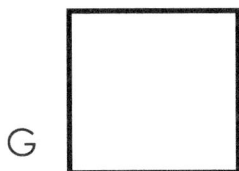

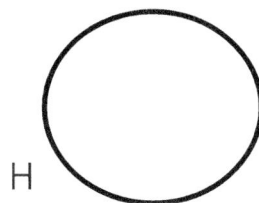

A

B

C

D

E

F

G

H

I

J

1. Name a common object that has the form of each of the vocabulary words

2. Which shapes represent the two dimensional shapes?

3. What are the names of the shapes G-J?

PORTRAIT TYPES

Sir Anthony Van Dyck Charles the 1st 17th

GLOSSARY	
full face	front view of the subject
profile	side view of the subject
three quarter	two-thirds view of the subject

1. Identify the portrait types A-F

2. How is shading creating three dimensional form in the sketches?

A   Raisa Berger, untitled 2015

B   Raisa Berger, untitled 2014

C   Raisa Berger, untitled 2014

D   Raisa Berger, untitled 2014

E   Raisa Berger, untitled 2015

F   Raisa Berger, untitled 2015

ANATOMICAL SKETCHES BY DA VINCI

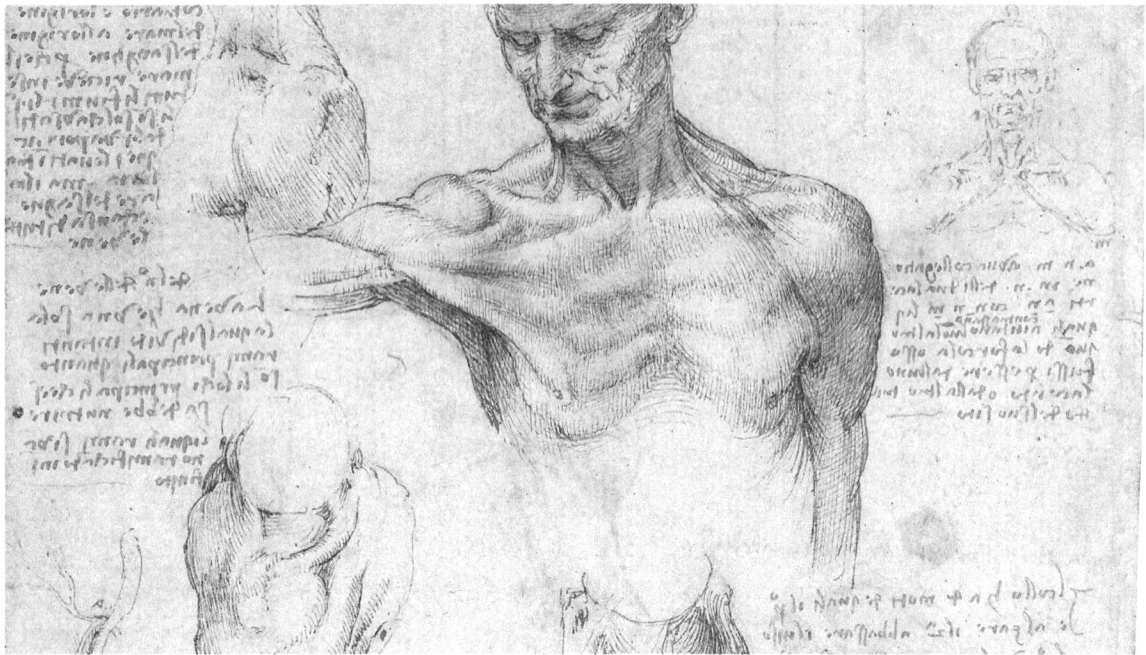

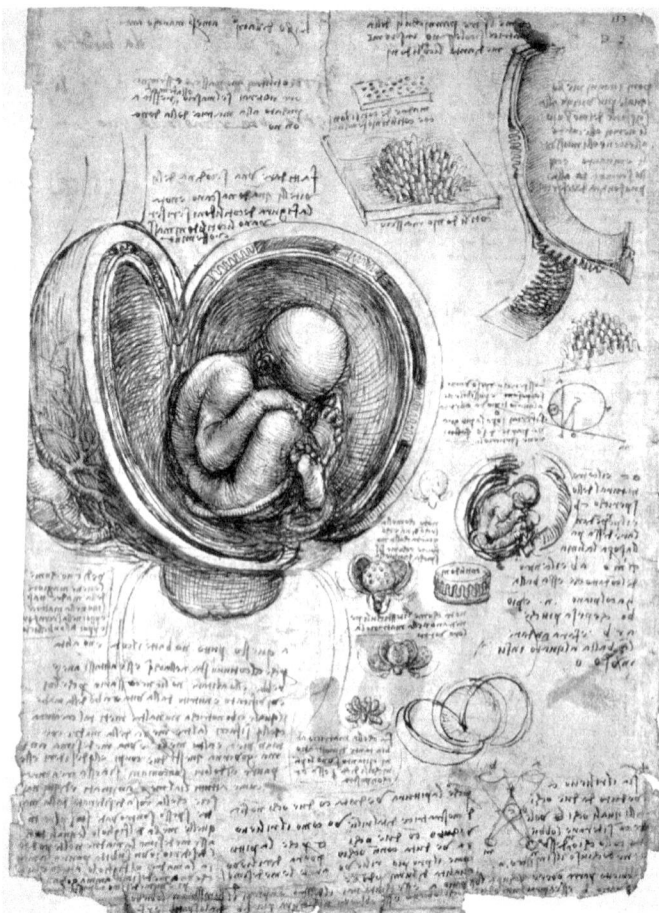

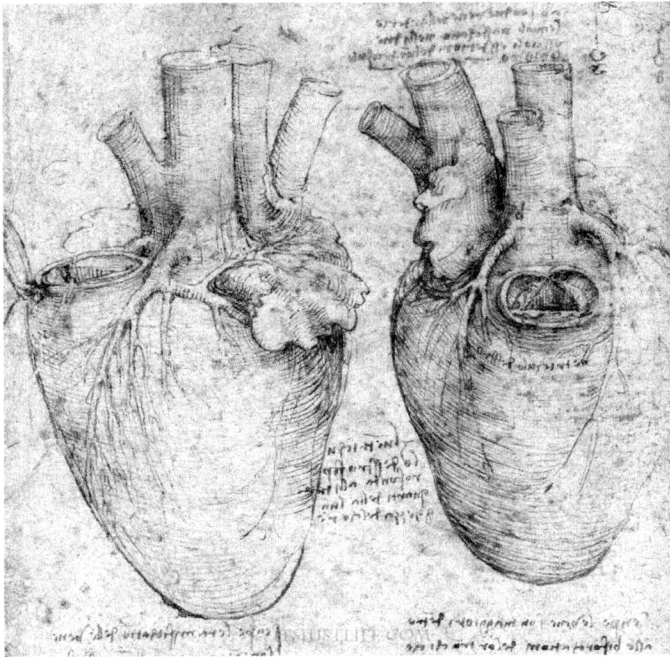

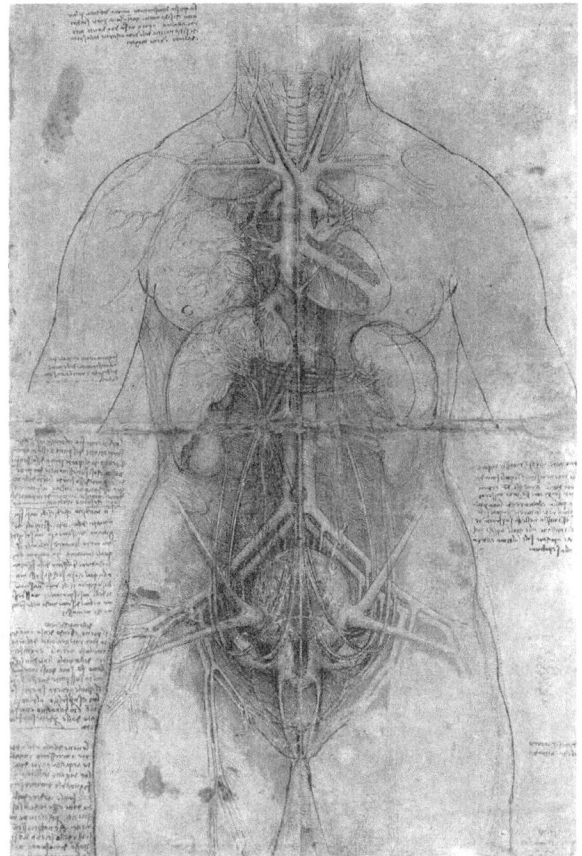

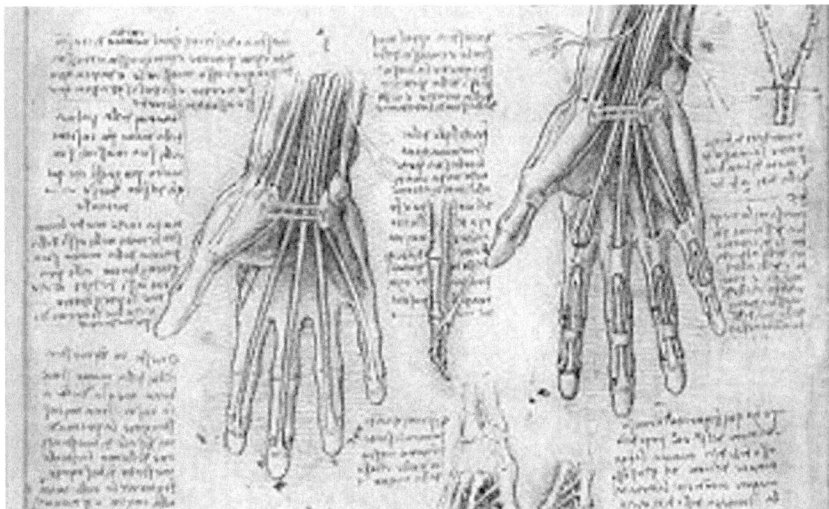

DISCUSSION

1. Da Vinci was an extensive note taker, what is the benefit of taking notes while working?

2. Da Vinci drew the human body from the inside out, why do you think that this was done?

3. How can studying anatomy make an artist more skillful?

4. What is your opinion of the working methodology of Da Vinci?

Leonardo Da Vinci, study 15th-16th

1. What is in the **foreground** of the sketch?

2. What is in the **background** of the sketch?

3. What is the **focal point** of the sketch?

4. What **focal point method** was used?

5. What is the **scene** in the sketch of?

6. What type of **balance** does the sketch have? Why?

7. What type of **rhythm** does the sketch have? Why?

8. What is your opinion of this **style** of sketch?

9. How is **harmony** represented with shapes?

10. Comment on the **emphasis** that the sketch has.

11. Comment on the **proportion**.

12. Comment on the type of **movement** that the sketch has and why.

13. How is **variety** used in the sketch?

14. Comment on the types of **line** techniques used.

15. Comment on how **form** is created in the sketch.

HOW TO SHADE BASIC FORMS
PENCIL TUTORIAL

ANSWER THE MULTIPLE CHOICE QUESTIONS

1. What creates the illusion of form?

    A. adding value to shapes   **B.** using highlights

    C. creating emphasis   **D.** adding color to shapes

2. What is usually the darkest area on the form?

    A. highlight   **B.** midtone

    C. core shadow   **D.** cast shadow

3. What shape does a square get turned into?

    A. a rectangle   **B.** a sphere

    C. a cube   **D.** a cylinder

4. What type of line comes down from the top of the diagonal

    A. vertical   **B.** horizontal

    C. straight   **D.** diagonal

5. The cylinder is drawn with an ellipse at the top and...?

    A. two horizontal lines   **B.** two zig zag lines from the el-lipse

    C. two vertical lines from each end of the ellipse   **D.** three lines, two straight and one crooked

6. What type of bottom goes on the cone shape?

    A. large   **B.** squared

    C. rounded   **D.** oval

Guess the famous painter based on the sketch.
How do they show form in their style?

A

B

C

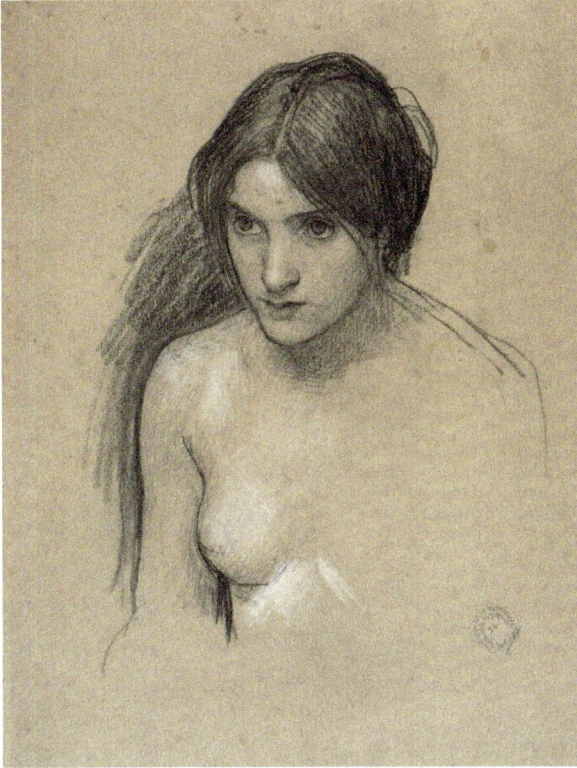

D

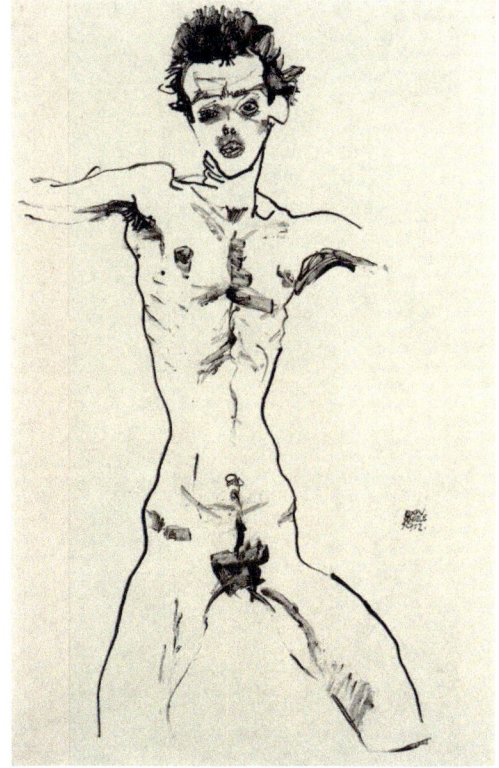

E

F

1. Egon Schiele, Self Portrait of an Act 1912

2. Egon Schiele, Girl 1918

3. Leonardo Da Vinci, untitled 15th-16th

4. Leonardo Da Vinci, untitled 15th-16th

5. John William Waterhouse, study for Hylas and the Nymphs 1896

6. John William Waterhouse, study in sanguine 1899

Hieronymus Bosch, Concert in the Egg 1566

SPACE

Space is any conducive area that an artist provides for a particular purpose. Space includes the background, foreground and middle ground, and refers to the distances or area(s) around, between, and within things. There are two kinds of space: negative space and positive space. Negative space is the area in between, around, through or within an object. Positive spaces are the areas that are occupied by an object and/or form.

SPACE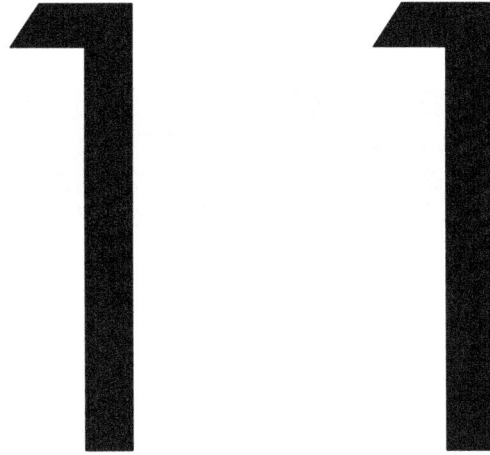

MUSINGS

1. What is the meaning of allegory?

2. What is the relationship between the words negative and positive?

3. What is the meaning of grotesque?

GLOSSARY

Early Nether-landish	the work of artists, sometimes known as the Flemish Primitives, active in the Burgundian and Habsburg Netherlands during the 15th- and 16th-century Northern Renaissance, especially in the flourishing cities of Bruges, Ghent, Mechelen, Leuven, Tournai, and Brussels, all in present day Belgium.
Flemish style	flourished from the early 15th century until the 17th century, gradually becoming distinct from the painting of the rest of the Low Countries, especially the modern Netherlands. In the early period, up to about 1520, the painting of the whole area is typically considered as a whole, as Early Netherlandish painting.
grotesque	the strange, mysterious, magnificent, fantastic, hideous, ugly, incongruous, unpleasant, or disgusting, and thus is often used to describe weird shapes and distorted forms
impasto	the process or technique of laying on paint or pigment thickly so that it stands out from a surface
triptych	a picture or relief carving on three panels, typically hinged together side by side and used as an altarpiece

FILL IN THE BLANK WITH THE CORRECT VOCABULARY WORD

1. "Ewwww! Close your mouth when you chew, that's _____!"

2. The Dutch artists from the 15th-16th century who worked in present–day Belgium are called _____.

3. He enjoyed running his finger along the canvas because he liked feeling the texture of the _____ paint.

4. The style that became distinct from Netherlandish style around 1520, called _____.

5. _____ is derived from the word "tri", which means three.

READING COMPREHENSION

1. What nationality was Hieronymus Bosch?

2. How many of his uncles were painters?

3. Why was the Brotherhood of Our Blessed Lady important for Bosch?

4. Why did the Netherlandish painters conceal their brushstrokes?

5. What is Bosch known for?

Hieronymus Bosch

Featured Artist

It is not certain when Jheronimus van Aken, better known as Hieronymus Bosch was born. His birthdate is placed sometime around 1450 and he was buried on August 9th 1516. Bosch was of Dutch nationality and he was born in the city Hertogenbosch. He was a painter who is part of the art movement known as the **Early Netherlandish** Renaissance. There are not many known records of the artist's life. Bosch spent all of his life in his hometown, Hertogenbosch. His grandfather, Jan Van Aken, was a painter. His grandfather had five sons. All of which were painters except for one. It is believed that either Bosch's father of uncle taught the artist how to paint.

In 1486 or 1487, Bosch joined the Brotherhood of Our Blessed Lady. The Brotherhood of Our Blessed Lady was an important social network for Bosch because his father was the artistic advisor for the brotherhood. Additionally, there were nobility as well as magistrates who also belonged to the brotherhood. The Netherlandish painters of the end of the 15th century and the beginning of the 16th century attempted to conceal their brushstrokes to suggest that their paintings were of divine origin. However, Bosch, would sometime paint in an **impasto** style. This was in contrast to the **Flemish style**. Bosch is known for his **grotesque** images and nightmarish, fiery depictions of hell, which could have been so realistic and frightening because he witnessed 4,000 houses burning as a youth. Bosch's body of work includes at least16 triptychs. Eight of which are still fully intact while five of them are in fragments. His most famous **triptych** is called The Garden of Earthly Delights. The Garden of Earthly Delights depicts very intricate symbols and scholars have come up with countless interpretations of the meaning of the painting over the centuries.

GLOSSARY	
background	the plane in a composition perceived furthest from the viewer
foreground	the visual plane that appears closest to the viewer
middle ground	the visual plane located between both the foreground and the background

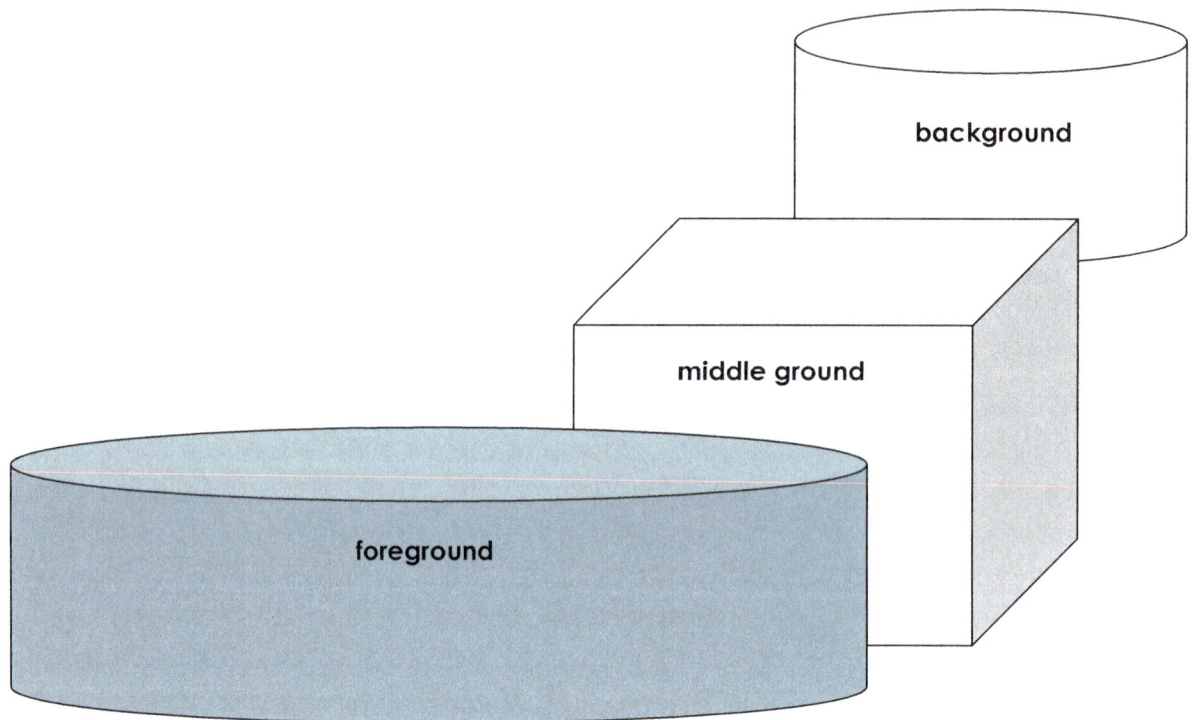

DISCUSSION

1. Which color represents the foreground in the painting?

2. Which color represents the middle ground in the painting?

3. Which color represents the background in the painting?

Hieronymus Bosch, detail from triptych of Saint Anthony 16th

GLOSSARY	
negative space	the area in between, around, through or within an object
positive space	the areas that are occupied by an object and/or form

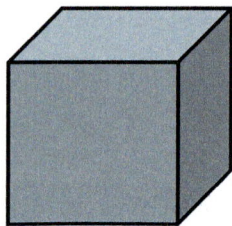

positive

negative

DISCUSSION

1. Which image represents the positive space in green?

2. Which image represents the negative space in green?

Hieronymus Bosch, Saint John the Baptist in the Wilderness 1489

Hieronymus Bosch, detail from triptych of Christ Carrying the Cross 15th

Hieronymus Bosch, Ship of Fools 16th

1. Comment on the foreground, middle ground, and background of each painting.

2. Comment on the negative and the positive space in each painting.

Hieronymus Bosch, Garden of Earthly Delights 15th-16th

DISCUSSION

1. The Garden of Earthly Delights contains many strange, allegorical images, do you think that you can guess the meaning of any of them?

2. What emotion do you think that the artist was trying to elicit from the viewer with these paintings? Why?

3. What is happening in the different "spaces" of the panels?

4. How is the artist using space?

5. Of the artists and art movements that we have studied this far, what art movement and/or artist does this painting style remind you of the most? Why?

LINEAR PERSPECTIVE IN ART

GLOSSARY	
horizon line	horizontal line that runs across the paper or canvas to represent the viewer's eye level, or show the area where the sky meets the ground
linear per- spective	a system of creating an illusion of depth on a flat surface. All parallel lines in a painting or drawing using this system, meet in a single vanishing point on the composition's horizon line.
perspective	representing three-dimensional objects on a two-dimensional surface in a way that looks natural and realistic; creates an illusion of space and depth on a flat surface
vanishing point	in a linear perspective drawing, the vanishing point is the spot on the horizon line to which the receding parallel lines diminish

DISCUSSION

1. What is depth?

2. What is in the foreground, middle ground, and the background?

3. Comment on the negative space and the positive space in the painting.

4. Do you think that the people located at the vanishing point are important? Yes or no and why or why not?

5. Why do you think that using linear perspective was common during this period of art?

6. What is located compositionally along the horizon line?

7. What does creating a *sense of depth* with linear perspective do to the composition?

Raffaello Sanzio Da Urbino, The School of Athens 1509-1511

horizon line

vanishing point

6 TECHNIQUES
TO CREATE SPACE

1. OVERLAP   Shapes that are closer, overlap shapes that are in the distance.

2. PERSPECTIVE   The use of one vanishing point can create depth.

3. PLACEMENT   Objects that are father away are placed closer to the horizon line

4. SHADING   The use of shading and shadow can make 2 dimensional objects appear to be 3 dimensional

5. SIZE   Objects that are closer to the viewer appear larger, whereas, objects that are far away appear smaller.

6. VALUE AND FOCUS   Objects that are farther away appear lighter and less detailed, whereas objects that are closer appear darker with more detail.

1. Locate an example in the painting showing **overlap**

2. Locate an example in the painting showing **perspective**

3. Locate an example in the painting showing **placement**

4. Locate an example in the painting showing **shading**

5. Locate an example in the painting showing **size**

6. Locate an example in the painting showing **value and focus**

Pietro Perugino, Christ Giving the Keys to Saint Peter 1481-1482

Hieronymus Bosch, An Angel Leading a Soul into Heaven 16th

1. What is in the **foreground** of the painting?

2. What is in the **background** of the painting?

3. What is the **focal point** of the painting?

4. What **focal point method** was used?

5. What is the **scene** in the painting of?

6. What type of **balance** does the painting have? Why?

7. Why is there **tension** in the painting? How is it created?

8. What type of **rhythm** does the painting have? Why?

9. What is your opinion of this **style** of painting?

10. How is **harmony** represented with shapes?

11. Are the colors mainly **high key**, **mid key** or **low key**? Why?

12. Comment on the **emphasis** that the painting has.

13. Comment on the **proportion**.

14. Comment on the type of **movement** that the painting has and why.

15. How is **variety** used in the painting?

16. Comment on the types of **line** techniques used.

17. Comment on the **color** technique used in the painting.

18. Comment on the **form** in the painting.

19. Comment on the **space** in the painting.

HOW TO DRAW USING ONE POINT PERSPECTIVE

ANSWER THE LISTENING COMPREHENSION QUESTIONS

1. What kind of line do you draw first?

2. What do you put in the middle of the horizontal line?

3. What do the horizontal lines do as they get closer together towards the vanishing point?

4. What is the first vertical line used for?

5. What is the triangle shape used for?

6. For one point perspective, how many vanishing points do you need?

7. What species of trees does the artist suggest drawing?

8. As things go away into the distance, what happens to them?

9. How can you change the tones of the lines to create one point perspective?

10. What type of line shows the height of the eye of the viewer of the image?

11. What reflections did the artist suggest could go into the river?

12. What makes the trees appear to "come forward"?

13. One point perspective is a very useful technique or device to create some sense of what?

14. The actual reality of the world is _____?

15. One point perspective makes things quite _____?

IMAGINING THE GROTESQUE IN ART

Hieronymus Bosch, Christ Before Pilate 16th

1. What's a story from literature that you can think of that has some negative elements, such as villains or evil characters? The story can be real or make believe.

2. Which characters would be represented in a grotesque way? Why?

3. What negative personality traits do the evil characters in your narrative have?

4. Can you think of a film that has grotesque characters? What is the film and who are the characters? What are their flawed personality traits?

Albrecht Dürer Coat of Arms with a Skull 16th

Jusepe De Ribera Large Grotesque Head 1617-1627

Peter Paul Rubens, The Head of Medusa 1617-1618

Michelangelo Caravaggio, Judith Beheading Holofernes 1599

VALUE

Value is used to create the illusion of light. Highlights and shadows combine to create the illusion of a light source. Value is the degree of lightness and darkness in a color. The difference in values is called contrast. Value can relate to shades, where a color gets darker by adding black to it, or tints, where a color gets lighter by adding white to it. White is considered the lightest value whereas black is the darkest. The middle value between these extremes is middle grey, which is also known as a half-tone, all of which can be found on a value scale.

VALUE 12

"All works, no matter what or by whom painted, are nothing but bagatelles and childish trifles... unless they are made and painted from life, and there can be nothing... better than to follow nature."
-Michelangelo Caravaggio

MUSINGS

1. What is your opinion on violent themes in art, music, movies, etc.,

2. What feelings are darkness associated with? Why do you think this is?

3. How can the value of a painting set the mood of a painting?

GLOSSARY	
Baroque	Followed Renaissance art and Mannerism and preceded the Rococo, and Neoclassical styles; art that flourished in Europe from the early 17th century to the mid 17th century.
chiaroscuro	in art, is the use of strong contrasts between light and dark, usually bold contrasts affecting a whole composition
Mannerism	also known as Late Renaissance, is a style in European art that emerged in the later years of the Italian High Renaissance around 1520, spreading by about 1530 and lasting until about the end of the 16th century in Italy, when the Baroque style largely replaced it
Naturalism	the attempt to represent subject matter truthfully, without artificiality and avoiding artistic conventions, or implausible, exotic, and supernatural elements. Realism has been prevalent in the arts at many periods, and can be in large part a matter of technique and training, and the avoidance of stylization
pupil	a person, usually young, who is learning under the close supervision of a teacher at school, a private tutor, or the like; student

FILL IN THE BLANK WITH THE CORRECT VOCABULARY WORD

1. The _____ technique creates a dramatic, moody atmosphere.

2. The _____ style of art followed the Renaissance art movement.

3. _____ was used in the painting. There were imperfections, which suggested real subjects were used.

4. The _____ had a lesson on contour line drawing that he really liked.

5. The _____ was replaced by the Baroque style of painting.

READING COMPREHENSION

1. Why did his family move to Caravaggio?

2. Who taught Caravaggio first?

3. Why did Caravaggio have to flee Milan?

4. What style of painting did the protestants prefer?

5. Who granted Caravaggio a pardon to return to Rome?

Michelangelo Caravaggio

Featured Artist

Michelangelo Mersi was born September 29th 1571 and he lived until July 18th 1610. Michelangelo Mersi is more commonly known as Michelangelo Caravaggio. He was born in Milan, Italy and briefly served as a knight. The name Caravaggio comes from the name of the town where his family moved to in 1576 to escape the plague that was ravaging Europe. A year later, he lost his father and grandfather to the plague. Caravaggio is associated with the **Baroque** movement of art. As a youth, Caravaggio was the **pupil** of Simone Peterzano. In 1592, Caravaggio had to flee Milan for Rome because of altercations with people, including a police officer. He arrived, poor, without money and without accommodations and he was in a very vulnerable position.

There was a lot of opportunity in Rome at that time because there were palaces and Catholic churches that were searching for a style that was different from the style that the protestants preferred, called **Mannerism**. Caravaggio was an innovative artist during this period due to his use of **chiaroscuro** as well as his use of **naturalism** in his style of painting. Caravaggio managed to form some important relationships with artists who would introduce Caravaggio to collects of art. Caravaggio's personal life, often complicated his career. He had a reputation for being a heavy drinker and a brawler. In fact, in 1606, he killed a younger man during a fight and he had to flee from Rome to escape the death penalty. Caravaggio fled to Naples and because of his fame, and his wealthy patrons with societal influence, Caravaggio managed to escape jurisdiction. He was on the run for some time and successfully persuaded the art-loving, Cardinal Scipione Borghese, the nephew of the pope of Rome, to grant him a pardon to return. Although he was successful and had many enemies by that time, he died of fever before he ever reached Rome.

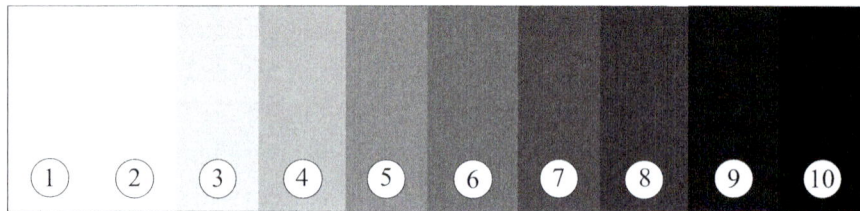

VALUE SCALE

1. Not all colors are equal in value (lightness or darkness).

2. Different values of the same color are called tints and shades

3. A shade is produced by adding black to a color.

4. A tint is produced by adding white to a color .

5. The number of values between white and black has been simplified to 1-10.

6. Not all colors are equal in value (lightness or darkness).

7. Value sets the structure of objects in paintings, not the color.

GLOSSARY	
high key val-ue range	values on the higher end of the scale
mid key val-ue range	values toward the middle of the scale
low key val-ue range	values towards the lower end of the scale

Claude Monet, Impression Soleil Levant 1872

John Sargent, A Dinner Table at Night 1884

Claude Monet, Grainstacks in the Sunlight Morning Effect 1890

DISCUSSION

1. Which painting demonstrates low key values?

2. Which painting demonstrates mid key values?

3. Which painting demonstrates high key values?

4. Which color on the wheel has the highest value? What about the darkest?

INCORRECT COLOR, CORRECT VALUE

Henri Matisse, Fruit and Coffeepot 1898

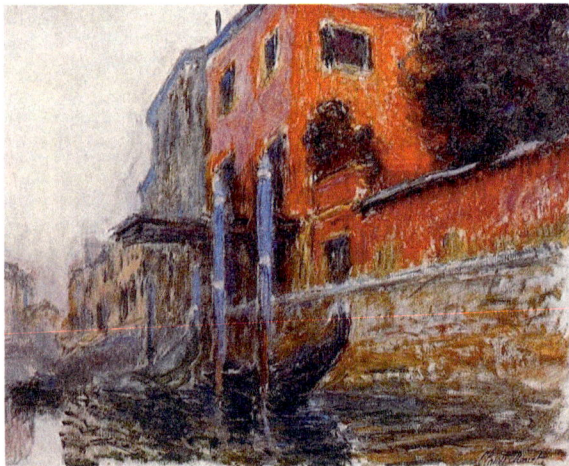

Claude Monet, The Red House 1908

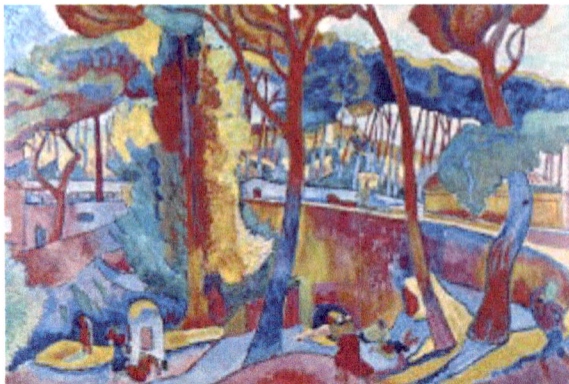

André Derain, L'Estaque 1905

GLOSSARY	
highlight	areas on an object where light is hitting
light source	area in which light is originating from
shades	dark values (colors combined with black)
shadows	areas on an object where light does not hit
tints	light values (colors combined with white)
value	element of art associated with the darkness or lightness of a color
value scale	a guide to creating a range of value, good pieces of art have a full range of value

DISCUSSION

1. Why might an artist experiment with unrealistic colors in their paintings?

2. How would an artist make sure that the unrealistic color had the same value as the realistic color?

3. What comments can you make on the color schemes of the paintings?

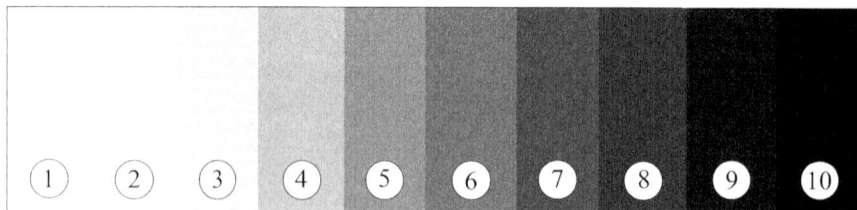

Michelangelo Caravaggio, The Taking of Christ 1602

DISCUSSION

1. Find areas with the corresponding values 1-10

2. Find an area with a highlight

3. Find an area with a shadow

4. Which way is the light source coming from?

5. Were low, mid, or high range values used in this painting?

Michelangelo Caravaggio, The Conversion of Saint Paul 1600-1601

Michelangelo Caravaggio, Saint Jerome Writing 1605-1606

DISCUSSION

1. What areas of the painting are emphasized with value?

2. Where does the light source appear to be coming from?

3. What areas in the painting are highlighted?

4. What other elements of the composition are dramatic?

Michelangelo Caravaggio, The Calling of Saint Matthew 1599-1600

Michelangelo Caravaggio, The Crucifixion of Saint Peter 1601

DISCUSSION

1. What areas of the painting are emphasized with value?

2. Where does the light source appear to be coming from?

3. What areas in the painting are highlighted?

4. What other elements of the composition are dramatic?

Michelangelo Caravaggio, Sacrifice of Isaac 1598-1603

1. What is in the **foreground** of the painting?

2. What is in the **background** of the painting?

3. What is the **focal point** of the painting?

4. What **focal point method** was painting?

5. What is the **scene** in the painting of?

6. What type of **balance** does the painting have? Why?

7. What type of **rhythm** does the painting have? Why?

8. What is your opinion of this **style** of painting?

9. How is **harmony** represented with shapes?

10. Comment on the **emphasis** that the painting has.

11. Comment on the **proportion**.

12. Comment on the type of **movement** that the painting has and why.

13. How is **variety** used in the painting?

14. Comment on the **color** in the painting.

15. Comment on how **form** is created in the painting.

16. Comment on the **space** in the painting.

17. Comment on the **value** in the painting.

CHIAROSCURO FORMS

ANSWER THE LISTENING COMPREHENSION QUESTIONS

1. What are the techniques that are covered for adding value to forms?

2. If light is coming from one direction, then the light and shadow will conform to a set of?

3. The area closest and most direct to the light is the?

4. As the light hits the object less directly, the value becomes?

5. What are the darkest areas called?

6. What area is between the cast shadow and the core shadow?

7. What type of pencil does the artist begin with?

8. Is the side of the lead or the point used to keep the transitions smooth?

9. What type of pencil is used to create the lightest tones?

10. What shows the highlight (where the light is hitting the sphere most directly)?

11. Which direction does the artist make the hatching lines go?

12. How do you control the lightness and darkness of the shape?

13. Where should the shadow fall?

14. How do you produce darker tones with stippling?

15. Why does the artist recommend using a marker for stippling?

CAMEOS OF THE ARTIST

Match the cameo with the situation from the life of Michelangelo Caravaggio

1. At some point the artist fell very ill and spent six months in the hospital. The painting indicates that it was likely malaria due to the jaundiced appearance of the skin, and the icterus of the eyes, which indicates that there were high levels of bilirubin.

2. An artist's envious and hateful attack on his enemy, which includes the face of his rival as that of the devil.

3. The second boy from the right, looking over his shoulder at the viewer.

4. The painting was sent to the papal court as a sort of petition for a pardon in order to return to Rome. The pardon was needed for the murder that was committed by the artist in 1606.

5. Blood spewing from the neck of the saint spells out the name of the artist.

Michelangelo Caravaggio The Musicians 1595

Michelangelo Caravaggio David and Goliath 1610

Michelangelo Caravaggio, Young Sick Bacchus 1593

Giovanni Baglione, Sacred and Profane Love 1601

Michelangelo Caravaggio, detail from The Beheading of Saint John the Baptist 1608

Tamara de Lempicka, Kizette in Pink 1926

SHAPE

Shape refers to a 2-dimensional, enclosed area, that is limited to being flat or limited to width and height. Shapes could be geometric, such as squares, circles, triangles etc. or organic and curvaceous.

SHAPE 13

"I was the first woman to paint cleanly, and that was the basis of my success. From a hundred pictures, mine will always stand out. And so the galleries began to hang my work in their best rooms, always in the middle, because my painting was attractive. It was precise. It was 'finished'."
-Tamara de Lempicka

MUSINGS

1. What were the four basic 2-d shapes that were learned in unit 10, form?

2. What is a polygon?

3. What does it mean if something is organic?

GLOSSARY	
Art deco	the predominant decorative art style of the 1920s and 1930s, characterized by precise and boldly delineated geometric shapes and strong colors and used most notably in household objects and in architecture
commission	a request by an individual, organization, or institution to an artist to create a specific artwork or project.
neo classical	was a Western cultural movement in the decorative and visual arts, literature, theatre, music, and architecture that drew inspiration from the art and culture of classical antiquity
self-portrait	a representation of an artist that is drawn, painted, photographed, or sculpted by that artist
still life (still lives)	a work of art depicting mostly inanimate subject matter, typically commonplace objects which are either natural (food, flowers, dead animals, plants, rocks, shells, etc.) or man-made (drinking glasses, books, vases, jewelry, coins, pipes, etc.

FILL IN THE BLANK WITH THE CORRECT VOCABULARY WORD

1. To create the _____, the artist used a mirror with three panels.

2. Bold shapes and strong colors are indicative of the _____ style.

3. The _____ contained apples, and a beautiful floral arrangement.

4. Some people think that the artist over-charged for the portrait that was _____.

5. Classical antiquity was the influence and inspiration for _____ art.

READING COMPREHENSION

1. What is Lempicka's style a combination of?

2. What did Lempicka do because of her hatred of the portrait?

3. Who was Lempicka trained with?

4. What is the name of the fashion magazine that used Lempicka's work as cover art?

5. Why did Lempicka and her husband travel to the United States?

Tamara de Lempicka

Featured Artist

Tamara de Lempicka, born Tamara Rozalia Gurwik-Górska, lived from May 16th, 1898 and she lived until March 18th, 1980. She was born in Warsaw, Poland. Lempika is known for her highly stylized **Art deco** paintings of nudes as well as aristocrats. She was trained by the painters Maurice Denis and André Lhote. Her painting style was a combination of cubism as well as **neo classical** style. Lempicka was inspired by the neo classical artist named Jean Auguste Dominique Ingres. Lempicka's father was an attorney and her mother was a Polish socialite. When Lempicka was only ten years old, she had a portrait **commissioned** of her by her mother to be completed by a prominent, local artist. Lempicka is said to have disliked the pastel portrait so much that she defiantly picked up the pastels and drew a portrait of her little sister, creating her very first portrait.

Tamara de Lempicka was formally trained at Saint Petersburg Academy of Arts and Académie de la Grande Chaumière with her sister. Her first paintings were **still lives**, portraits of her daughter Kizette, and her neighbors. By 1925, Lempicka was gaining recognition and exhibiting work in major venues as well as fashion magazines. One of her most famous works is a **self-portrait** titled, *Tamara in a Green Bugatti,* which appeared on the cover of a German fashion magazine, *Die Dame*. In 1929, Lempicka traveled to the United States for work and shortly afterwards, her career began to flourish. Her works began to be shown amongst influential artists, she painted royalty, and her work was being shown in museums. Due to World War 2, Lempicka and her husband moved to the United States where they settled in Los Angeles, California. She continued to paint celebrities, still lives, and even **abstract** paintings in the 1960s. She would live out the large majority of the rest of her life in the states, until 1974, at the age of 76, when she move to Cuernavaca, Mexico. Upon her death six years later, she had the ashes of her cremated body strewn into a local volcano.

ADVANCED GEOMETRIC 2-D SHAPES

GLOSSARY	
crescent	a shape that is curved, wide at its center, and pointed at its two ends like a crescent moon
decagon	a flat shape with ten straight sides and angles
ellipse	a shape that resembles a flattened circle : oval
hexagon	a flat shape that has six angles and six sides
heptagon	a flat shape that has seven sides and seven angles
nonagon	a flat shape with nine straight sides and nine angles
octagon	a flat shape that has eight sides and eight angles
pentagon	a flat shape that has five sides and five corners
semi-circle	a shape that is half of a circle or of its circumference

Match the form to the vocabulary term A-I

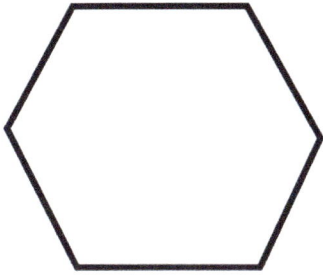

A

B

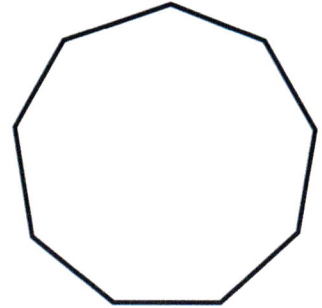

C

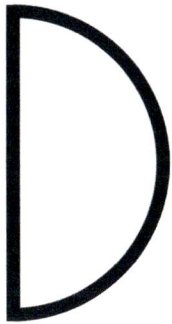

D

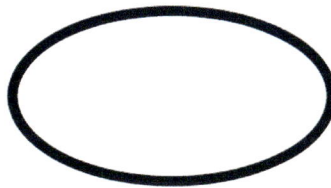

E

F

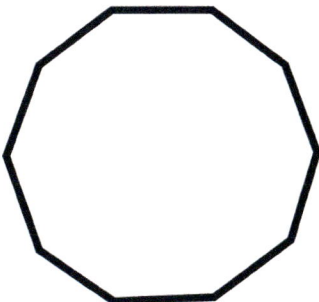

G

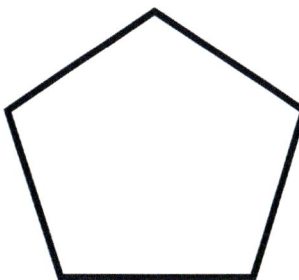

H

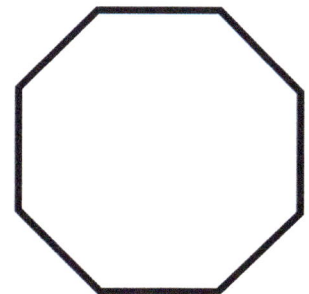

I

GEOMETRIC SHAPES VERSUS ORGANIC/FREE-FORM SHAPES

GLOSSARY	
geometric	a geometric shape can be defined as the form of an object or its outline, outer boundary or outer surface
organic (free-form)	irregular, uneven, or unpredictable and flowing in appearance.; these shapes, as well as organic forms, visually suggest the natural, plants, sky, sea, etc.

ORGANIC SHAPES

1. What paintings have geometric shapes? In what parts?

2. Which paintings have organic shapes?

3. Which painting doesn't have any geometric shapes. Why?

4. Is the human body geometric or organic? Why or why not?

Michelangelo Caravaggio, Amor Vincit Omnia 1601-1602

Robert Delaunay, Rythme Joie de vivre 1930

Wassily Kandinski, Composition 8 1923

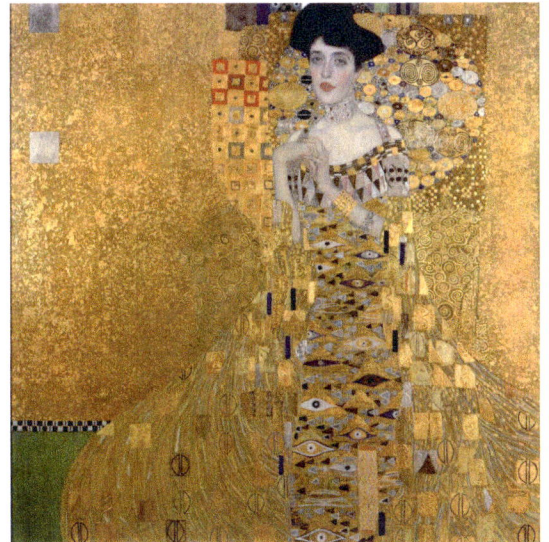
Gustav Klimt, Portrait of Adele Bloch Bauer 1903-1907

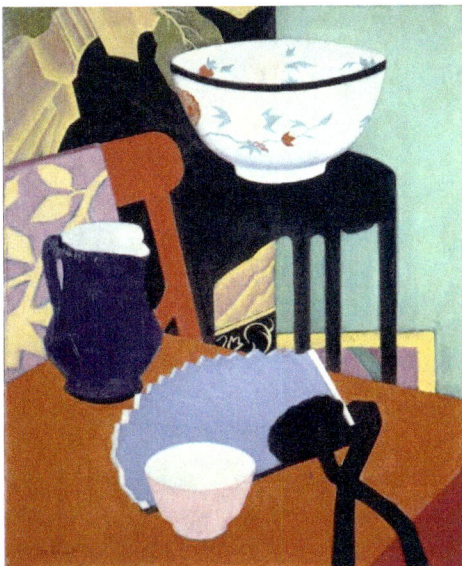
Francis Campbell Boileau Cadell, The Blue Fan 1922

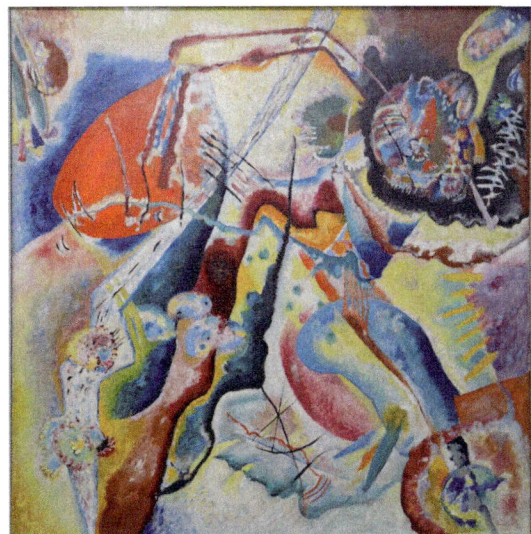
Wassily Kandinski, Tableau Latach Rouge 1913

Tamara de Lempicka, Il Fondo Rosa (Portrait of Bibi Zögbe) 1923

Tamara de Lempicka, Double 47 1924

DISCUSSION

1. What shapes do you notice in the paintings?

2. How does the placement of the shapes impact the overall composition of the paintings?

Tamara de Lempicka, portrait of Marquis Sommi 1925

1. What is in the **foreground** of the painting?

2. What is in the **background** of the painting?

3. What is the **focal point** of the painting?

4. What **focal point method** was painting?

5. What is the **scene** in the painting of?

6. What type of **balance** does the painting have? Why?

7. What type of **rhythm** does the painting have? Why?

8. What is your opinion of this **style** of painting?

9. How is **harmony** represented with shapes?

10. Comment on the **emphasis** that the painting has.

11. Comment on the **proportion**.

12. Comment on the type of **movement** that the painting has and why.

13. How is **variety** used in the painting?

14. Comment on the **color** in the painting.

15. Comment on how **form** is created in the painting.

16. Comment on the **space** in the painting.

17. Comment on the **value** in the painting.

18. Comment on the **shapes** in the painting.

TAMARA DE LEMPICKA - THE LIFE OF AN ARTIST

ANSWER THE MULTIPLE CHOICE QUESTIONS

1. Tamara De Lempicka was a refugee from

   A. Ukraine   **B.** Syria

   C. Thailand   **D.** Russia

2. The _____ masters inspired Tamara De Lempicka and greatly influenced her art.

   A. Chinese   **B.** French

   C. Italian   **D.** Parisian

3. Who was De Lempicka taught by at the academy?

   A. Maurice Dennis/André Lhote   **B.** René Magritte

   C. Pablo Picasso   **D.** Maurice Dennis/Van Gogh

4. In 1929, another portrait of Kizette at her first communion won a _____ medal at the International exhibition in Poznań.

   A. platinum   **B.** gold

   C. silver   **D.** medal

5. **What did the Hollywood stars refer to De Lempicka as?**

   A. the socialite of Paris   **B.** the baroness with the brush

   C. the painter with the charm   **D.** the baroness with the talent

6. In 1960, she began to use a _____ knife.

   A. brush   **B.** sharp

   C. palette   **D.** collector's

It is possible to locate basic shapes in the individual components of a composition as well as the overall components of the composition.

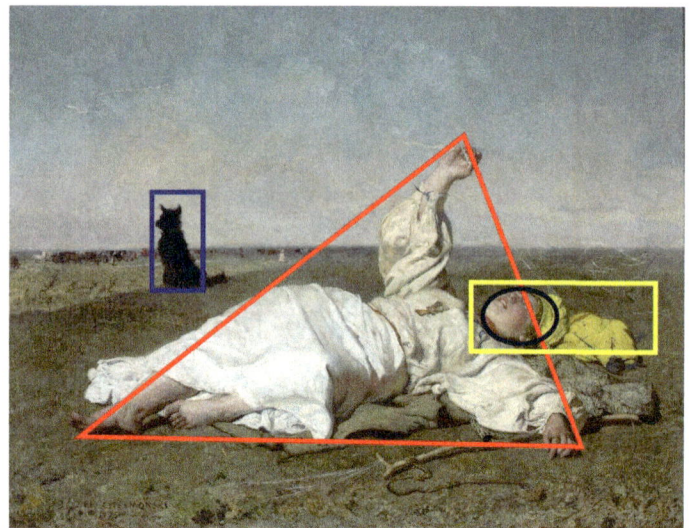

Józef Chełmoński, Indian Summer 1875

1. Comment on the individual basic geometric shapes in each painting.

2. Comment on the overall compositional shapes that are created in each painting.

3. Which of the paintings has organic shapes?

4. What objects create the organic shapes?

Jan van Eyck, The Arnolfini Portrait 1434

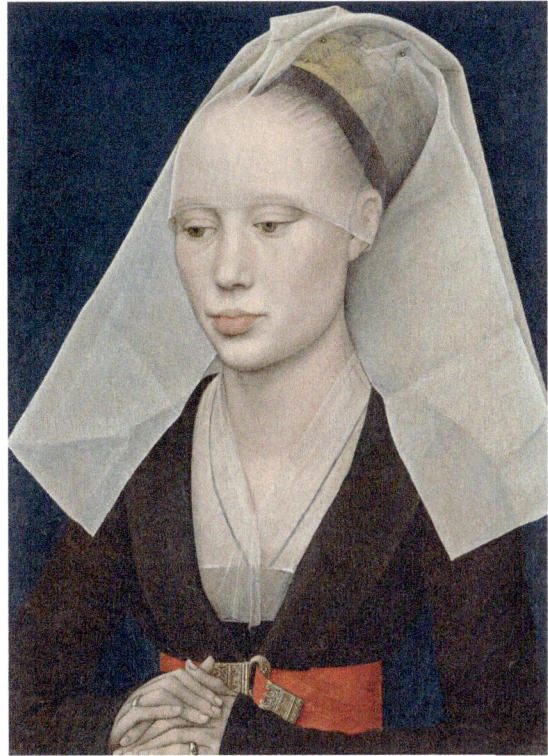

Rogier van der Weyden, Portrait of a Lady 1460

Tamara de Lempicka, Irene and her Sister 1925

Martin Johnson Heade, A Vase of Corn Lilies and Heliotrope 1863

Georges Seurat, Farm Women at Work 1883

TEXTURE

Texture, another element of art, is used to describe the object more and how something feels or looks. A small selection of examples of the descriptions of texture are furry, bumpy, brittle, smooth, rough, soft, and hard. There are many forms of texture; the two main forms are actual and visual.

Visual texture is strictly two-dimensional and is perceived by the eye that makes it seem like the texture.

Actual texture (tactile texture) is one not only visible, but can be felt. It rises above the surface transitioning it from two-dimensional to three-dimensional.

TEXTURE 14

MUSINGS

1. Do you enjoy being able to see the brushstroke of the artist in paintings? Yes or no and Why or why not?

2. How can brushstrokes contribute to the mood of a painting?

3. What some words for different types of textures?

GLOSSARY	
divisionism	also called chromoluminarism , it was the characteristic style in Neo-Impressionist painting defined by the separation of colors into individual dots or patches which interacted optically
modern art	from the 1860s to the 1970s, and denotes the styles and philosophy of the art produced during that era. The term is usually associated with art in which the traditions of the past have been thrown aside in a spirit of experimentation
mono-chrome	also called monochromatic; painting that is created using only one color or hue; it can use different shades of one color, but by definition should contain only one base color
pointillism	a technique of neo-impressionist painting using tiny dots of various pure colors
Post impressionist	a predominantly French art movement that developed roughly between 1886 and 1905, which was from the last Impressionist exhibition up to the birth of Fauvism. The movement emerged as a reaction against Impressionism and its concern for the naturalistic depiction of light and color

FILL IN THE BLANK WITH THE CORRECT VOCABULARY WORD

1. The _____ painting was made up of various shades and tints of blue.

2. Because the painting was made in 1955, it was included in the _____ exhibit.

3. _____ is the painting technique of painting tiny dots on a canvas.

4. The period of art in France after the last impressionistic exhibit in 1886 was the _____ movement.

5. The _____ painting technique combines tiny dots of paint, which create optical color illusions.

READING COMPREHENSION

1. Who taught Seurat in 1878?

2. What did Seurat do as part of training at the École des Beaux-Arts?

3. How long did Seurat serve in the military?

4. What is the name of the scientific writer that influenced artists?

5. What was Seurat very invested in?

Georges Seurat

Featured Artist

Georges Seurat was born on December 2nd 1859 and he lived until March 29th 1891. The cause of his death is uncertain, but, it seems to have been an infectious disease because his son died two weeks after the death of his father. Seurat was born in France in the city of Paris. He was a **Post impressionist** artist. Seurat first studied art at the École Municipale de Sculpture et Dessin. The sculptor, Justin Lequien, ran the school. In 1878, Seurat joined the École des Beaux-Arts where he was taught by Henri Lehmann. There, Seurat got a conventional academic training, which consisted of drawing from casts of antique sculptures and copying the drawings of the old masters. During Seurat's education, he would learn artistic theories that he would later use to guide his artistic methodologies. Seurat's formal artistic education ended in 1879 when he left the École des Beaux-Arts for a year of military service.

After his military training, Seurat moved back to Paris and shared a studio with his friend, Aman-Jean, where he mastered the technique of **monochrome** painting. Michel Eugène Chevreul was a 19th century scientific writer who influenced many artists of the time with his writings on color , optical effects, and perception. **Pointillism** and **divisionism** come from Chevreul's theory that two colors that are close together would have the effect of another color when seen from a distance. Seurat was very invested in color theory and a scientific approach to painting. He believed the scientific approach to painting would naturally lead to paintings that were harmonious. It seems as though the artworld agreed with Seurat's methodologies because his large scale piece, A Sunday Afternoon on the Island of La Grande Jatte (1884–1886), changed the direction of **modern art** and brought in neo impressionism. In fact, the painting is seen as one of the most iconic paintings of the 19th century.

The 3 Types of texture

GLOSSARY	
ephemeral	fleeting forms which are changing such as clouds, liquids, smoke, flames, etc.
optical	the skillful painting technique that creates the illusion of the texture of the painted object on the canvas
physical	the expressive brushstrokes of the artist; the physical texture conveys the emotional energy of the artist and the subject

1. What type of texture(s) does the *Starry Night* painting have?

2. What type of texture(s) does the *Bouquet of Flowers in an Urn* painting have?

3. What type of texture(s) does the *Zlatovláska* painting have?

4. What type of texture(s) does the *Still Life with a Flower Garland and a Curtain* painting have?

5. What type of texture(s) does *The Shipwreck* painting have?

6. What type of texture(s) does *The Banjo Lesson* painting have?

Vincent Van Gogh, Starry Night 1889

Jan van Huysum, detail Bouquet of Flowers in an Urn 1724

Viktor Olivia, Zlatovláska 20th

Adriaen van der Spelt, Still Life with a Flower Garland and a Curtain 1658

Joseph Mallord William Turner, The Shipwreck 1805

Henry Ottawa Tanner, The Banjo Lesson 1893

Unit 14 TEXTURE   247

Evert Collier, A Vanitas 1699

Christoffel van den Berghe, Still Life with Dead Birds 1624

PAINTING MULTIPLE SURFACE TEXTURES

bumpy	fluffy	rough	silky	sticky
coarse	glossy	sandy	slick	wet
cold	hairy	scaly	slimy	wispy
dry	hard	scratchy	smooth	wrinkly
feathery	prickly	shiny	soft	velvety

DISCUSSION

1. Which adjectives for texture would you use to describe objects in the Evert Collier painting?

2. Which adjectives for texture would you use to describe objects in the Cristoffel van den Berghe painting?

3. What additional adjectives can you think of to describe the textures in either of the paintings?

Georges Seurat, A Sunday on La Grande Jatte 1884

DISCUSSION

1. Comment on the texture of the *A Sunday on La Grande Jatte* painting.

2. What feeling does the texture method give the painting?

3. What is your opinion on the texture method used for the scene?

4. How does the technique on the painting on the left differ from the painting technique on the right?

Georges Seurat, La Mer a Grandcamp1885

DISCUSSION

1. Comment on the texture of the *La Mer a Grandcamp* painting.

2. What feeling does the texture method give the painting?

3. What is your opinion on the texture method used for the scene?

4. Which of the two painting techniques do you feel is more aesthetic? Why?

Georges Seurat, Bathers at Asnières1884

1. What is in the **foreground** of the painting?

2. What is in the **background** of the painting?

3. What is the **focal point** of the painting?

4. What **focal point method** was painting?

5. What is the **scene** in the painting of?

6. What type of **balance** does the painting have? Why?

7. What type of **rhythm** does the painting have? Why?

8. What is your opinion of this **style** of painting?

9. How is **harmony** represented with shapes?

10. Comment on the **emphasis** that the painting has.

11. Comment on the **proportion**.

12. Comment on the type of **movement** that the painting has and why.

13. How is **variety** used in the painting?

14. Comment on the **color** in the painting.

15. Comment on how **form** is created in the painting.

16. Comment on the **space** in the painting.

17. Comment on the **value** in the painting.

18. Comment on the **shapes** in the painting.

19. Comment on the **texture** in the painting

GEORGES SEURAT – A SUNDAY ON LA GRANDE JATTE
(1884-1886)

ANSWER THE MULTIPLE CHOICE QUESTIONS

1. How many years did Georges Seurat work on the painting?

    A. 1 years   **B.** 3 years

    C. 2 years   **D.** 4 years

2. Where did the last private owners donate the painting?

    A. The Institute of Atlanta   **B.** The University of Chicago

    C. The University of Art   **D.** The Art Institute of Chicago

3. What type of grid was used to arrange the composition?

    A. 4X4   **B.** 3X5

    C. 3X3   **D.** 5X5

4. What does the last plane of the painting contain?

    A. a girl running toward a trash can   **B.** a woman fishing

    C. a monkey   **D.** foliage and sky

5. What is the name of the ancient building with the friezes that inspired the figures of the painting?

    A. the Ara Pacis   **B.** the Colosseum

    C. Saint Peter's Basilica   **D.** the Panathenaeans (Parthenon) by Phidias

6. Some people think that the painting depicts

    A. different social classes who hang out together in the same places   **B.** the feelings of people about the government

    C. the artist's feelings about wealthy people   **D.** the park, which is well manicured

Trompe-l'œil

Trompe-l'œil paintings became very popular in Flemish and later in Dutch painting in the 17th century arising from the development of still life painting.

- **trompe-l'œil**   French for "'deceive the eye'") is an art technique that uses realistic imagery to create the optical illusion that the depicted objects exist in three dimensions.

- **verisimilitude**   The appearance of being real

In the 5th century BC, a man name Zeuxis staged a contest with a fellow artist to see who could paint the most realistic painting. He competed with an artist called Parrhasius. When Zeuxis revealed his painting, it was so realistic that birds flew down from the sky and tried to peck at the grapes that were in the drawing. Then, Parrhasius told Zeuxis to reveal his painting by pulling back the curtain, but was shocked to see that the curtain was actually a part of the painting. The curtain itself was an illusion. Zeuxis then exclaimed that, "*I have deceived the birds, but Parrhasius has deceived Zeuxis!*"

DISCUSSION

1. Which of the trompe-l'œil paintings looks the most realistic to you, why?

2. What do you think the meaning of the Escaping Criticism painting is? Why?

3. Do you believe that the contest between Zeuxis and Parrahasius really happened? Why or Why not?

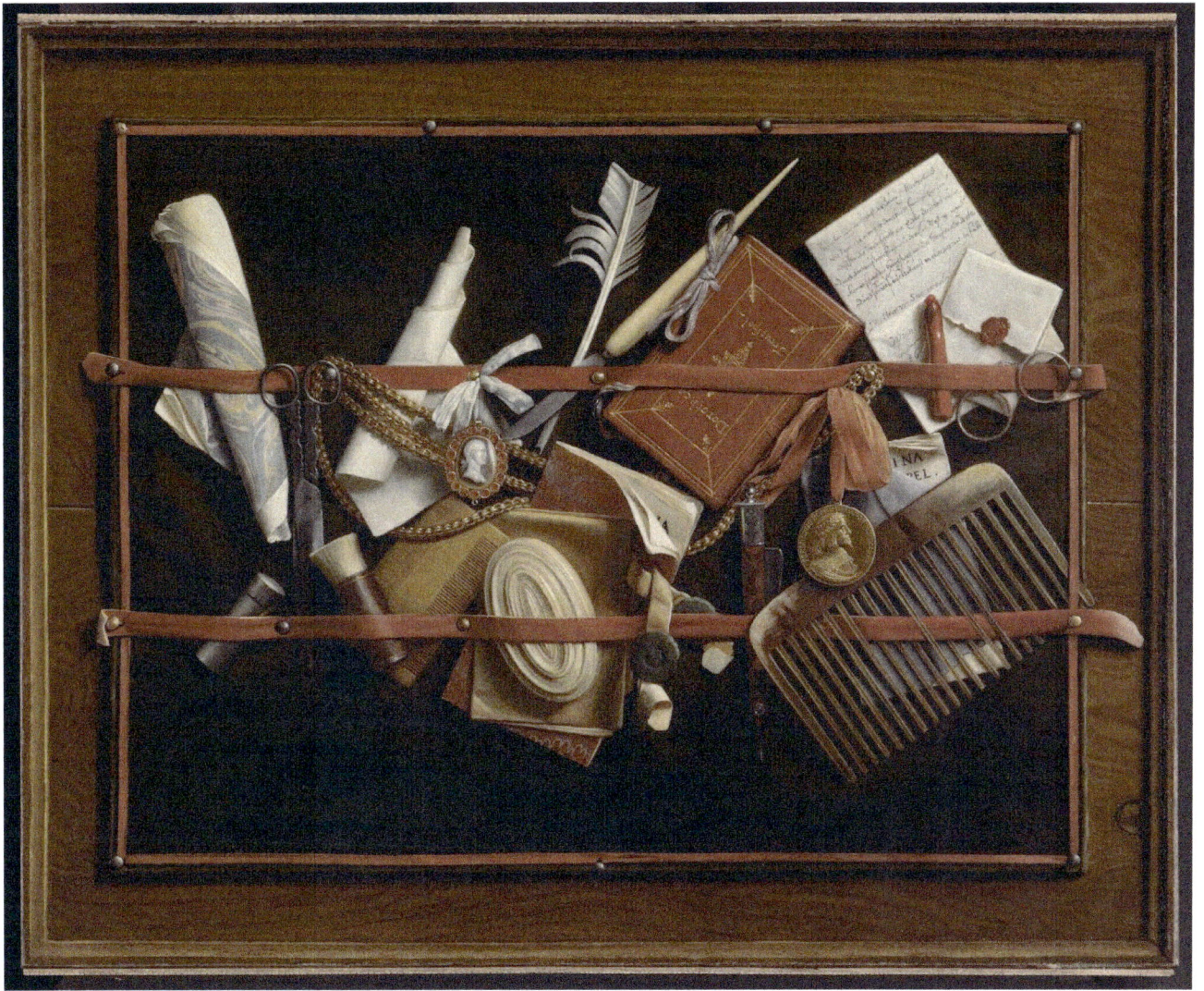
Samuel van Hoogstraten, Still Life 1666-1678

Pere Borrell del Caso, Escaping Criticism 1874

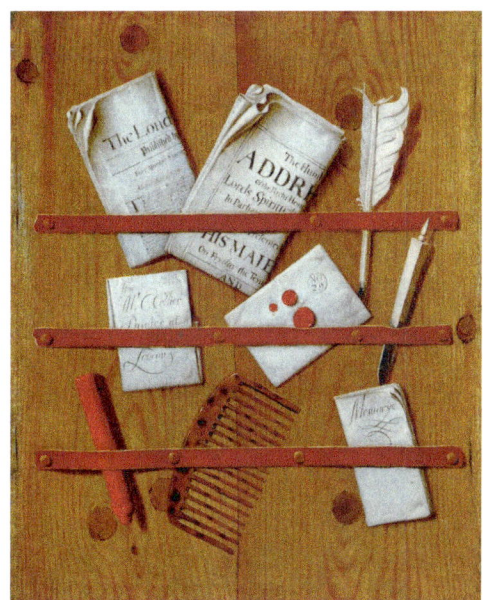
Evert Collier, Newspapers, Letters, & Writing Implements, 17th

"Have no fear of perfection, you'll never reach it." -Salvador Dali

Printed in Great Britain
by Amazon